THE BOOK STARTS HERE

How To Publish Your Story

Reini Schühle & Karl Woolley

Yorkshire Art Circus
1996

Published by	Yorkshire Art Circus
	School Lane
	Glasshoughton
	Castleford
	WF10 4QH
	tel: 01977 550401
	fax: 01977 512819
	e-mail: BOOKS @ ARTCIRCUS.DEMON.CO.UK
© Text:	Yorkshire Art Circus and the authors
	The extracts in Section Six are taken from current and past Yorkshire Art Circus books.
© Cover Image:	Jackie Fenton-Elliott (Snakes and Ladders)
Cover Design:	Paul Miller @ ergo design
Writing Team:	Reini Schühle, Karl Woolley
Readers:	We are grateful to John Armitstead, Charlie Wallace, Roy Bedford and Jo Henderson for 'road-testing' this book, and to Dave Goldthorp, Lorna Hey, Clare Conlon, Ian Daley; also to Brian Lewis and Nigel Milner for their professional advice.
Typesetting:	Reini Schühle, Art Circus Education
Printing:	FM Repro, Roberttown, Liversedge
ISBN:	1 898311 24 2
Classification:	Library Science & Publishing

British Library Cataloguing in Publication Data.
A catalogue record for this book is available from the British Library.

Yorkshire Art Circus is a unique book publisher. We work to increase access to writing and publishing and to develop new models of practice for arts in the community.

Please write to us for our full programme of workshops and our current book list.

Yorkshire Art Circus is a registered charity No 1007443.

Yorkshire Art Circus is supported by:

Yorkshire & Humberside Arts, West Yorkshire Grants, Wakefield MDC Leisure

CONTENTS

INTRODUCTION

If you are considering writing your story - or have completed writing it - and you are looking for ways of getting published we hope this book will help you. The reader we have in mind is someone wanting to publish their life story although we feel that *The Book Starts Here* is also useful if you want to publish other forms of writing. If your main motive is to get rich quick we suspect this is not the book for you but if you are mainly interested in getting your writing more widely known, then read on.

Yorkshire Art Circus is a community publisher. We run our own publishing programme and offer publishing advice across our region as well as training here at Glasshoughton. We provide direct access to publishing for a small number of first-time writers through our own books programme and give practical advice on how to present a manuscript. For writers who live locally and who want to self-publish we offer support at our resource centre.

Over the years we have responded to numerous letters and phone calls from writers who are looking for a publisher. There is clearly a need for a practical guide to getting published, to self-publishing and, especially where we are dealing with autobiographical writing, to good writing and editing.

The transformation is magic. What started off as a collection of notes and went through stages of progress and desperation takes on an identity of its own. No wonder the author feels it is like giving birth, with the publisher as midwife to the book.

The Book Starts Here is a first port of call. It gives you practical information but by its very nature it has to be general. As well as giving answers, it will also raise quite a few questions. The section at the end points you towards further information. There is no point re-inventing the wheel so there are sample forms for you to adapt to your own project. The little boxes along the main text contain additional information, appropriate quotes or points we feel are worth reinforcing. Many of these points are based on the experiences shared with us by writers and community groups we have supported into publishing or into getting published.

We hope you enjoy this book. Dip into it for background information or use it to guide you through the ups and downs of publishing.

Section One

GETTING PUBLISHED

Vanity publishing

How to get published

How to present your work to a publisher

How to present your manuscript

They have accepted: contracts, royalties, copyright, tax

In the widest sense, anyone who has produced a text that can then be read by other people is a publisher. A publication can exist in a 'run' of one, or a print run of ten thousand or more, or anything in between. You may well feel that writing is what you are good at and what you want to do, and you are happiest to leave publishing to others. We will look at your options but only fairly briefly. This book is mainly about self-publishing.

Vanity publishing -

one woman's experience

I had written my life story and was keen to get it published. I didn't know a lot about publishing; to be honest, I knew nothing. The small ad in one of the Sunday papers looked promising. I wrote off; an impressive looking catalogue came by return post and after they'd seen my manuscript I received a very flattering letter. They'd be pleased to take on my book. I'd have to pay but not to worry, this would be foolproof; their marketing and distribution service would sell my books in no

I photocopied my father's typed-up life story three times and had each copy bound. At Christmas I gave him the three bound copies. 'This,' I said, 'is now published in an edition of three.'

time and leave me with a tidy little profit. It all looked very professional and reputable. Here was my chance to use my savings for something I really wanted to do and make money to boot. Two years later: I have paid the production bill of £8000 for 1000 books and so far I have received £23 in sales income. They didn't promise too much; it really was foolproof. I just didn't realise who the fool was!

If your publisher asks you for a contribution towards publishing costs beware. We've all seen the adverts which announce, 'We want your stories! We will publish your manuscript. All you need to do is send us some money!' They seem very tempting.

The touts who advertise and sell you their 'services' call it by more attractive and imaginative names but when you are asked to pay to be published you are probably dealing with vanity publishing. It is what it says. It plays on our vanity and exploits our burning desire to be published. A proper publisher will take the complete financial risk either because they are pretty sure that it will pay off in book sales or because they are keenly aware of the quality of the writing and feel strongly that your text deserves a wider readership. A vanity publisher need have no scruples over quality. Their main income is not from book sales but from the fee they charge you, the writer, for printing your text. Often the contract does not even oblige them to produce bound copies; you could well end up with a pile of printed, collated pages but with no covers. Being slightly more optimistic, you might end up with a thousand copies of your book but no intention on the part of the vanity publisher to do the hardest bit: promoting and selling your book for you.

After a three-year legal battle author Joanna Steans won a rare victory against a 'vanity' press. They had to repay her in full since the book they produced using her money was 'of such poor quality that it is unsaleable.'

Ask yourself why they should. The percentage of the cover price which goes to the publisher as net profit tends to be 5% to 10%. For a £4.99 book that means a return to the publisher of 25 to 50 pence - a modest return on quite an investment.

Vanity publishing means cutting the labour-intensive and risky bits out of publishing; there is no need to build up an editorial policy or develop a longer-term relationship with authors. As long as there are writers desperate to get published and convinced that self-publishing is too complicated for them, vanity publishers will flourish.

People should be paying *you* for your efforts so let's waste no more time on vanity publishing.

How to get published

From the first it is important to make the distinction between a printer and a publisher. A printer performs a mechanical task for money; printers print and produce books or pamphlets. Very occasionally, printers publish, usually they do not. Publishers publish: they work out a publishing policy and programme. They negotiate with authors, edit, deal with designers and printers, promote and market the books, set up accounting systems, plan and, most importantly, take the risk. Last but not least, they pay their authors.

There are two main routes into conventional publishing:

1- You approach someone else, a publisher, to take over and to produce, market and distribute your text on your behalf. You have two choices: either you find a publisher or you find an agent who will then find a publisher on your behalf.

2- You publish yourself. Quite a few famous authors started off by publishing their work because nobody else would, so you will be in good company.

The agent

The agent's job is to know what is going on in the publishing world and to be your advocate. Since the agent does this for a living there must be some financial reward. Different agents work in different ways. The most current *Writers' & Artists' Yearbook* or the *Writer's Handbook* both have lists of agents with a summary of the types of writing they handle and whether they accept unsolicited manuscripts, and also an indication of their conditions. Finding an agent is not easy, especially not for an unpublished writer; understandably, agents tend to want to work for authors who already have a track record.

It's the same with agents as with anything else: you get what you pay for!

How to pick a publisher

Publishers have a wealth of publishing policies. They range from the *purely* commercial to other reasons, including a need to keep old traditions alive, a wish to add to the diversity of the book culture, or promote a particular type of writing, or get new writers read.

There are many small presses with a variety of publishing programmes based on locality, race, gender or specific culture.

Unfortunately very few publishers will touch a full length manuscript by an unknown writer and 90% of manuscripts will end up on the slush pile. There are lots of reasons for this:

• the manuscript is too similar to one they have just published which didn't sell
• the manuscript is too similar to one by a better known author already on their list
• the sheer volume of manuscripts received
• the author is not well enough known
• the standard of writing is poor
• the standard of presentation is poor
• the manuscript is unsuitable for this publisher

Some of these reasons are beyond your control; the last three you can definitely do something about.

A common complaint from publishers and editors is that the manuscript doesn't fit in with the programme of that particular publishing house. The culprits tend to be unsolicited manuscripts since agents will send a particular manuscript to the most appropriate publisher.

The Oxford English Dictionary definition: fiction, n. Feigning, invention; thing feigned or imagined, invented statement or narrative, especially novels

Before you consider which publisher to approach, you have to know where your book fits into the market. If you have written a children's book you should narrow your search to publishers who have children's books in their programme. If their programme includes fiction but not poetry you would be wasting your time and theirs by sending your collected poems.

So the first thing is to get hold of the most current edition of the *Writers' & Artists' Yearbook* or of the *Writer's Handbook* in the library and plough through.

The publisher's name is usually followed by a short description of what type of texts they publish. Note down the publishers who deal with your type of text.

Once you've narrowed down your possibilities, do some practical research:

• Get catalogues for your chosen publishers.
• Go into a good book shop or library and look at books by your chosen publishers.
• Which of their books are available?
• Which books are on the best seller shelf?
• Which autobiographies are being promoted (if yours is a life story)?
• Will you need to angle your story in a particular way?
• Are similar books in the library well read? Check the date label.

How to present your work to a publisher

Put together a well-constructed proposal. This looks more professional than just your manuscript. A proposal should consist of:

1. A brief covering letter including a CV
2. The synopsis (summary) of your text
3. Sample chapters
4. A self-addressed, stamped envelope
5. A self-addressed, stamped post card if you want the publisher to confirm that your proposal has arrived with them.

The covering letter

Keep the covering letter and CV to the point. Publishers know that we all have to start somewhere but a track record can help confirm your professionalism: if you

The story came to us as a manuscript of half a million words. The author had been encouraged to write but nobody had bothered to tell her she would be extremely unlikely to find a publisher for that size of book by an unknown author.

have had any writing experience or success mention it but don't waffle on about how your friends think your writing is good or exciting. Only mention possible sales outlets if you can be specific and certain. Be very careful with illustrations, especially drawings. Unless they are an integral part of your writing they are an unnecessary variable. The publisher might be put off by them and not read your text.

The synopsis

Publishers are usually more worldly wise than writers. They have the necessary critical distance to a piece of writing. Their initial decisions are based on the synopsis and the sample chapters, therefore a clear and concise synopsis is vital.

A synopsis is a summary of what your book is about. It is worth spending some time on your synopsis - it is the first contact the publisher will have with you. A well written synopsis increases the chance of your sample chapters getting read rather than binned or returned. Writing a synopsis is a useful exercise for any writer - if you have problems writing it, your readers are likely to have problems reading your text too!

It doesn't matter how you have actually written your story, whether you have started with a plan, a skeleton which you have then fleshed out with your story, or whether your writing has taken shape in a more organic, maybe less conscious, way. Once the story is finished it will reveal its structure if it is well written. The structure may be expressed through a clear story line or through patterns of behaviour or speech, or through recurring imagery. Alarm bells begin to ring if a synopsis is overlong and confused; a good synopsis reveals the structural back bone of good writing.

Your synopsis should be accompanied by a word count. As well as the theme/s of the book the synopsis should introduce the characters and setting/s and give a very brief chapter-by-chapter summary. The shorter and the more concise your synopsis, the more likely it will be picked up and actually read.

The manuscript came through the post. Two weeks later there was an irate phone call asking why we had not contacted the author. We had to point out that we needed not only return postage but also his name and address.

The sample chapters

The beginning of your story is crucial; it needs to draw the reader in and make them want to turn the pages. It is essential that you enclose your first chapter or the first part of it. The other chapters need to be chosen so they guide the publisher through and give the best possible idea of the full text.

If a publisher asks for a synopsis and a set number of chapters or a set number of pages it is best to comply with their directions as much as possible. If you don't, you risk that your submission won't even be looked at.

How to present your manuscript

If you have already chosen a particular agent or publisher it's worth checking with them how they would like your writing to be presented. Generally manuscripts must be

- typed/wordprocessed on A4 paper,
- double-line spaced,
- on one side only,
- with wide margins,
- with page numbers,
- with title page with name, address and where possible phone number
- fastened together securely

Always send copies, do not send originals.

The final paragraph of a recent submission letter to us ended: 'If you are not hooked by this time, dear reader, we are both wasting our time.' This is very true. Publishers deal with a great number of proposals every day, some interesting, some boring and some indifferent. Your synopsis must make the publisher want to read your full story. It's the first hurdle your manuscript has to clear on the way to publication.

The manuscript had no page numbers. The typing went right to the edges of the page, the lines were close together. It would have required a saint to read it without feeling some resentment.

The long wait

Once your text has been dispatched you can forget all about it. There will now be a long wait and you may as well get started on another piece of writing. Publishers are inundated with material. You may not hear anything for six months or so. Like most businesses publishers have to plan well ahead. Their programme for the next couple of years will be fixed so that even if you get a positive reply there is still a long time to go before you hold your book in your hands.

If you haven't heard within three to four months send a polite reminder.

They have accepted

Be prepared to have to compromise. There may be cuts and alterations; your idea of a title or of the look of the book may be discarded. Only you can know how you weigh up becoming published against losing control over your work. The choice is yours, there's no universal right or wrong.

Recently we received a 500,000 word autobiography which we knew we had to get down to 60,000 words. Working together with the author, our editor re-fashioned the text to suit our list and our production budget.

The author knew it wasn't going to be the book she had written but since she realised that it would be a better book she chose to go with our proposal.

Contracts

Most writing benefits from 'snipping and pruning' by an editor. The author is so involved with the writing that they find it difficult to see the wood for the trees.

Usually a publisher will give you a contract at this point. It will specify what they will do in terms of production/distribution/marketing/promotion, what they expect of you the author in terms of promotional support (book signings, readings), and what you will get paid. It may set out who has editorial control. The contract will also stipulate who has control over the copyright and for what period of time.

If you are a member of the Society of Authors or the Writers Guild of Great Britain they will check your draft contract. An agent would also do this for you. If you seek legal advice make sure you talk to a specialist in contracts and copyright.

Royalties

Don't be misled by the Jeffrey Archer deals. Big sums upfront are the exception. It's more normal that you will get a cut on each copy sold. This is called royalty. Royalty percentages vary between publishers and for different types of publication. On publication, some publishers give an advance on royalties. In addition to the five free copies publishers give writers as a matter of course some small presses may prefer to give you extra copies of your book in lieu of royalties.

Copyright

Copyright protects the form rather than the underlying idea - just as well, since there are only about seven plots from which humanity constructs its stories. The idea in your head has no protection but once you have written it, your text will automatically be copyright-protected. Using a publisher does not mean you have to let go of your copyright. Often authors assert their copyright on the verso page of the book by putting *copyright: the author* and by putting: *The moral right of the author has been asserted.* You can also use this wording when you self-publish.

Tax

It is easy to forget or overlook but if you make income out of your writing, or out of self-publishing, you need to declare your earnings after deduction of expenses. Get some professional advice first. There may be travel, materials, typing fees and other legitimate expenses. Check what expenses you can offset against any income. If you receive a grant find out from the grant-giving body whether it is chargeable to income tax or not.

I signed the contract. My royalties will be just under 10% of the cover price on each book sold. If the full print run of 1000 sells out I will be £500 better off. It's not millionaires' row just yet but it's a start.

Section Two

PUBLISH YOURSELF

Self-publishing

Consider your options

Your reasons

Your market

Your resources/cash flow

Costs

If you get rejection slip after rejection slip but you are still convinced that your writing ought to be published, consider self-publishing. This may be the most sensible option in any case, especially for small print runs and a very localised market. We will continue to assume that you are not in it for the money; you will be happy if you break even but you don't expect to make a profit. And just as well. Your best realistic aim is to recoup the printing and marketing costs; if you also manage to pay yourself for your writing you will have done extremely well.

'I trust I shall never more feel ambitious to see my name in print; if the wish should rise, I'll look at Southey's letter, and suppress it.'
(Charlotte Brontë
to Southey who had sent her
a crushing review)

Self-publishing

Admittedly a pinch of vanity is part of any form of publishing, self-publishing included. But self-publishing is about much more: enterprise, skill training and fun. It is a legitimate form of publishing where the publisher just happens to be the same person as the author.

People are sometimes put off self-publishing because they see it as a form of vanity publishing. There is a big difference. Vanity publishing cynically exploits our desire for recognition or fame irrespective of the quality and the selling potential of the writing. If you are honest with yourself as self-publisher there are no false hopes raised or impossible promises given in return for hard-earned cash. You are also in good literary company with the likes of William Morris, Virginia Woolf, William Blake, Timothy Mo and a host of modern Soviet Russian writers. Your main motive is wanting your writing more widely read. This gives you far greater flexibility - you are not quite the slave to unit costs and economies of scale as someone motivated largely by profit margins.

Self-publishing is well-suited to niche markets. A commercial publisher is restricted to large print runs; you can cater in a much more flexible way for markets from one reader upwards.

Consider your options

Before you leap into action pause and think about
• your reasons for wanting to publish
• your potential market and distribution options
• resources and costs

The decisionmaking process that determines whether and how you publish is anything but linear. Each decision has an impact on the others. There is no clean-cut, straightforward route for your decision. It will involve jumping ahead, backtracking and moving sideways, modifying your earlier decisions and making several decisions simultaneously - an intellectual game of *Snakes and Ladders*. This is no reason to give up, it's just a reminder to keep an eye on the whole picture.

Reason I writing this book now is everlasting looking back, remembering things that happen, what life like as I progress through. I know just what must go in. Maybe things from my life some use to younger people. It not a lot I can do, I an ordinary man, but what I know, I did not learn in books, I did learn from living it!
Alfred Williams,
To Live It Is To Know It

Your reasons

There are lots of valid reasons for wanting to get published: fame, fortune, passing on family history, explaining yourself to others, telling a tale. There is nothing wrong with ambition; if you are convinced that you should be up there with the best-sellers, go for it. There are recent examples of writers who were convinced that they should have been published and who managed to prove that they were right by successfully going it alone.

There is an opportunity to be successful but there is also a risk of losing out financially. Make sure that you keep your risk manageable. Your reasons will help you determine your potential readership and the look of your book; good planning will minimise your risk-taking.

Recently an author was dropped from their list by a large bookshop chain because he no longer fitted their marketing profile. This finished him off since he needed his book to sell in the tens of thousands to survive as a writer. It was a real Catch 22: he needed to sell through the chain to reach high sales figures, the chain needed him to sell in high figures before they'd reconsider.

Your market

Do you really need to think about the market for a book? Doesn't everybody read books? You'd be surprised how many people there are who want to bring out a book of their own writing but when asked, 'Do you buy books?' they answer, 'No.' Do a quick spot check among people you know. Find out how many books they've read over the last year, and, more importantly, how many they've bought. This can be quite a sobering experience.

Boxes of your book languishing unsold and unsaleable under your bed represent a waste of your money and are a soul-destroying publishing experience. To choose your best option you need a clear idea of your market and how to reach it. Your market has a direct impact on the type of book you produce and on the print run.

Knowledge is strength. What follows is a broad, general overview of the book market as a whole and is intended as background information that will underpin your decisions.

The book market

Despite the recession, book production has increased; a staggering 95,000 books were published in 1995, of which roughly 40,000 were new titles. This means more competition for publishers, headaches for retailers in deciding which books to stock but also more choice for the consumer.

In Britain, over three quarters of books are sold to individuals as opposed to institutions, with the largest increase in reference books in hardback and scientific, technical and medical books in paperback, and generally in 'how to' manuals. Buying books as gifts and impulse buying are important factors in the book market with a wide range of books competing.

Who buys books?

- About a quarter of us never buy books.
- When people do buy books they tend to buy more than four books in a year.
- The young buy more than the old.
- Women are the real book buyers.
- Generally, people in the south are better book buyers, maybe due to affluence and commuting patterns. The location of bookshops is also important.

Book sales are influenced by genre, geography, product and market trends:

Genre

Different types of book appeal to different types of people. To find out what the markets are, look at individual publishers of that genre. The monthly *Bookseller* magazine is a good source of information about trends and target markets.

Geographical and cultural differences

Not all books have national appeal, a local history book will mainly sell in the locality to which it refers although there will also be an 'exile' market of people who have moved away. There are local cultural differences: Rugby League for example is popular in Yorkshire/Lancashire but not as much in other regions.

*How many books have you bought in the last year?'
I asked.
'None, I write books,' came the answer, 'I don't read them.' Why should anyone want to publish an author who doesn't buy or read books?*

Technology

CD-ROMs represent serious competition, especially to reference books, in the future.

Commercial practice

The abolition of the Net Book Agreement may have an effect on how and who publishers sell and promote their books to. Instead of selling the book at the printed cover price shops can now decide what they charge. The signs are that the implications will take some time to affect small print runs, or localised markets.

Where do people buy their books?

• Over half of those buying books in book shops have bought from WH Smith's. They seem to target a younger market, the 20 - 24 age group in particular although signs are that they are moving away from selling books.

• Professional, affluent people tend to buy books from a wide variety of outlets, including specialist book shops like Dillons or Waterstones.

• White collar workers tend to buy through book clubs.

• Manual workers and those at the lowest levels of subsistence are least likely to buy from book shops, they tend to buy from confectioners, tobacconists and newsagents, and also from book clubs.

Marketing is about spotting a need and meeting it through your product. It's about getting across to your customers the benefits your product will bring to them if they buy - rather than its features.

Researching your market/distribution

Market research is a very important consideration. Everything else depends upon it. Your market will have an impact on your print run. The quicker you identify your market, the quicker you can start planning and promoting your book. Against the background of the general market trends you need to assess the potential of your particular book.

Do some market research which is specific to the book you have in mind. This research will help you identify who are the most likely buyers and how you can reach them, whether through direct contact or commercial outlets.

• Look around the shops to see if your intended type of book sells well.
• Note the cost of similar books.
• Ask people if they would buy a copy of your book.
• Set up a subscription scheme.

The outcome of your research won't be very accurate but it will point you in the right direction. It's better to make an educated guess than to stumble along in the dark.

Your resources/cash flow

These come in three main forms:
• People time
• Materials, skills, support in kind, equipment
• Cash

People time

If your aim is to publish rather than to make a profit or earn a living, this is an important resource. You can put in your time unpaid and do many of the jobs for which a commercial publisher would need to pay: writing, typing, editing, proof reading, typesetting, printer liaison, promotion, repping, book keeping.

Materials, skills, support in kind, equipment

To do your own typesetting you need desk top publishing equipment - a personal computer and dtp software. If you don't own the right equipment it may be

I couldn't find a publisher for my illustrated walks in the Lakes so I did it myself when I retired. I learnt how to desk top publish and to negotiate with printers, got marketing advice, set up distribution and took it from there. I've published two books so far. Although I haven't made any money I haven't lost any either. I'm happy, I've achieved what I set out to do.

possible to get access to training and equipment. Most local authorities now run computer courses. Some give access to their computers outside teaching time. You may also find ways of getting materials or services at cost or free. The more you can do yourself the less cash you need.

Cash

Unless you actually have access to a printing press the point will come when you have to buy services and you need to pay, most likely in cash. This is the hardest resource to locate.

You will need to pay the production costs for your book long before you get the first sales income.

Unless you have some money saved up and you are prepared to risk it you need to raise cash. Fundraising is quite a specialised field and outside the scope of this book. Here are some of the options you could explore other than getting a bank loan. Remember to check the tax implications:

Subscription
Ask your would-be readers to pay for the book before it's produced. It's a good way to gauge your potential market. Subscription will show what interest there is in your book. It's also a good way of promoting your book in advance. Give out a form which tells about the book and offers it at a reduced price if people subscribe and pay before publication. This removes some of the financial risk by giving you a contribution to your printing costs upfront. If your time scale allows, your subscribers could have their name printed in the book to acknowledge their support. *(There is a sample subscription form on page 80.)*

You must have a good accounting system in place to make sure that subscribers get their paid-for copy; there will be a time lapse of six months at least between subscription and printed book. If you don't get a good enough subscription response and decide not to publish you must return the advance payments.

I didn't have enough cash for the print bill but luckily I had enough good mates willing to share the risk with me. The book was printed and sold out. I didn't make any money but I paid everybody back.

Shares

Instead of subscribing to the book your share holders put in a chunk of money, £50 or £100. After deduction of publishing costs the author or publisher receives a considerable share of the sales income because of their work. Each share holder is then entitled to a proportion of the remaining sales income which relates to how much they put in originally. The beauty is that the shareholders only have a small - although real - risk. They are essentially underwriting the publication. It's not the most foolproof way to become a millionaire but it's a very direct way to support arts in the local community.

The following options are probably much more uncertain but you may want to consider them:

Grant support

You may be able to apply for a grant either to your local council or to your Regional Arts Board. *(For addresses see page 77.)*

Sponsorship

Try local businesses. They usually want to do something for the local community; your book may just fit the bill.

Grant support or sponsorship mean you may have to give up some editorial control to meet the requirements of your funders - they will want their logos in and they may also want a say on the contents.

Cash flow

Whichever way you hope to raise the cash to fund your book, plan your cash flow.

Your designer and printer want paying within 30 days of sending you their invoice. Your sales income won't materialise until at least two months after publication. You need some money to bridge this gap. If you sell through shops there are two further considerations:

We went to a well-known high street shop with our begging bowl. There was no way they would give us money; requests for financial support had to go to head office in triplicate at least nine months in advance. What they could offer was support in kind. It was one headache less for us and the biscuits served at this launch were distinctly superior!

1- Shops will want a cut, a 33% discount is still standard but the bigger shops may well want 40%, with WH Smith's taking at least 48%.

2- Shops will take your books on sale or return. This means that you don't really know how many you have actually sold until after the specified sales or return period which could be 60 days or whatever you agree with the shop. Some of the bigger shops then take 3 months processing the sales information before they finally pay you.

Take these points into consideration when you work out your cash flow. They will also have a bearing on your cover price.

Costs

We are assuming that you have managed to deal with some of the production costs by doing the work yourself. So we'll ignore editing, typing, proofing, page lay-out, page design and typesetting. This still leaves you with cover design and printing costs and, after publication, with publicity/promotion, book sales administration and distribution costs.

Design costs

For one book we have recently been quoted £800 and £1800 by two printers who had both been sent identical specifications. They were going to deliver to the same standard so our choice was easy!

The cover is vital in selling a book. Apart from sales to people who know you and buy for that reason, your book will sell - or fail to sell - by its cover. An attractive, eye-catching cover increases the chance for your book to be given shelf space in the shops so don't make false savings here. Get a professional designer in to help you.

The more different designs you get your designer to work up the larger their fee will be. You can keep the design costs down by giving your designer a clear brief and by limiting the number of design options you require.

Printing costs

There are two main components:

1- Paper costs: these go up in line with the print run. Paper costs fluctuate, ask your printer to shop around.

2- Setting up costs - getting the presses ready and getting the text onto plates from which it can then be printed: these costs are roughly the same for one book as for 10,000. The printer has to set up the press irrespective of the numbers of copies to be printed.

This means that in very small print runs the proportion of setting up costs will be very high. Most of the printers we work with would not recommend print runs of less than 300 - the unit cost per book will be quite high.

If you know you could sell 100 books but no more, you'd have to work out if it's worth getting the minimum 300 printed and fixing the cover price so that your production costs can be recouped.

If you know that you could only shift 20 books then you need to consider different production methods.

For print runs of 300 and over you now need to find a printer. Word of mouth is a good starting point. Ideally you want a printer who is local, has experience in printing and producing books, can accommodate small print runs and delivers on time.

Shop around. Send a specification sheet to several printers setting out the job you want them to do. It is vital to compare prices. The variation between two printers can be quite staggering. Allow some time to shop around; speak to other publishers to find out who they recommend. Ask to see examples of the printer's work, preferably books similar to the one you want to publish, to be sure they are up to the job. If you are not happy with the quotation ask for explanations. This is the first step towards a good working relationship. It's your hard-earned cash and if you are going to spend it with a printer you need to feel confident that you will get your money's worth. *(There is a specification sheet on page 79.)*

Computers have been instrumental in the second revolution in book production. The first came about when movable print was invented, giving more universal access to books and to reading.

Publicity/promotion costs

Once your book exists, you need to let potential customers know. The costs here are of the 'how long is a piece of string' variety. If you have time and skills and media contacts you can save money. Your minimum costs will be for sending out free review copies to the media.

Book sales and distribution costs

Your market research will have helped you work out your print run. You can then work out how you will get your books to your readers. How you do this depends on many factors:

- Print run: if you have a small number of books you can probably sell them yourself through subscription and face-to-face selling.

- Your time commitments: if you have time you can set up your own limited distribution.

- Your intended market: the more local your market, the easier it is for you to do your own distribution.

- Your inclination: If you enjoy self-promotion you will find this easy but not everyone is good at selling, especially selling their own work. Rejection can feel like a personal judgment rather than a commercial and therefore profit-driven decision by a shop.

If you want to sell through shops you need to get the books to them before the publication date; they will not pay for your postage and packing. If you sell mail order direct to the public, you have administration costs setting up a reliable system but at least you can either charge for postage and packing separately or you could incorporate that cost in the cover price.

All these costs make up your unit cost and will have a bearing on your cover price.

The media love quirky stories. One of my books was cited positively in a court case. The local paper printed the story and from there it went up to the nationals. This free publicity has rekindled interest in my book and brought in new orders.

Section Three

YOUR BOOK

One-off books, Short runs of books, Larger print runs

Cover design

Page design

Book size

Binding

The price on the cover

Having your writing turned into a book by a printer costs a great deal of time and money, particularly if you wish to sell your book to a wider audience. But if you really want something just for family and friends you should reconsider the cheaper alternatives. There are many ways of becoming world famous round here!

A single copy may be read by more people than something which is printed in hundreds, languishing unsold at the back of book shops or under your bed. Writers through the ages have circulated their manuscripts among friends. Shakespeare circulated his 'sugred sonnets' so if you want to see it that way, he was a self-publisher. This method suited him, maybe it would suit you?

All the following methods depend on a well-typed copy of your text. The best solution here is to desk top publish. There is computer software that will let you set your text in a choice of type faces, with a variation of point sizes. You can also design your page lay-out to fit different sizes of page. Make sure you get a very clear printout, ideally off a laser printer. A double-sided printout will look more book-like than single-sided copy.

A couple of years before he died, Jack was himself being photographed outside his home. A passer-by looked quizzically on. 'It's all right,' Jack explained. 'I'm Jack Hulme. I'm famous, you know. World famous round here.'
World Famous Round Here - The Photographs Of Jack Hulme

One-off books

This is the one copy, or the short run of up to five or ten. Your production techniques could be quite elaborate, depending on what your aim is: are you simply providing reading matter or are you creating a special object in book form at the same time? There are adult education book binding classes if you want to do it all by yourself, or you could use a professional book binder to bind your text to your specifications. Depending on how much you are prepared to spend you can have different types of binding, from leather to cloth. One simply bound A4 size book with 120 pages will cost you in the region of £20.

Use this option if all you want is to have some copies just for your family or friends.

It's good for up to ten copies. If you want more copies you'll have to start looking into cheaper binding options, maybe using heat seal binders or stapling your books with home-produced card covers. Stapling limits the possible number of pages - over 40 pages could mean that the book won't shut properly.

Short runs of books

At this point you need good photocopying facilities. For one-offs you can use computer printouts, for print runs over ten you will have to move into photocopying as the cheaper option.

The resource centre helped me to edit and typeset my story but they could only offer heat seal binding. I thought my text deserved better so I went on a short book binding course at the Adult Education Centre and produced my own bound copies.

There are many different combinations:

• photocopied inside, handmade cover

• photocopied inside, photocopied cover

• photocopied inside, computer colour-printed cover

• photocopied inside, cover printed by a printer

• laser printed inside on DocuTech, cover printed by a printer

Larger print runs

Once you go over a run of 100 you enter a twilight zone in production: Print runs below 300 carry very high unit costs, so printing isn't the ideal solution; photocopying and hand-producing on this scale is tedious, variations in quality will be difficult to control. New technology allows for compromise: for print runs of over 100 you could opt for a printed cover but laser printed text using DocuTech. Some professional printers offer this option as one of their services.

Once you exceed 300 copies, check with your printer for the best method of production. If you need to distribute through commercial sales outlets you also need to ensure that your book can compete in a commercial setting.

Cover design

Don't let your publication down: design to a book is like the sound track to a movie. Good design - both cover design and page design - will enhance and complement your writing and give it the setting it deserves. This applies whether you produce one copy or a large print run. For all publishing options you need to spend some time on producing a book people will want to pick up and read. The book needs to look appealing, the text inside needs to be set out so that it invites the reader. Make sure that certain ground rules are adhered to: the title must be legible, the cover image must support the title. Make your design either outrageously different or play safe with a format other publishers have tested before you. Imitation is the sincerest form of flattery. Looking at other publishers' books will set you on the right path.

Impulse buying is an important factor in book purchasing. Ask yourself how *you* buy books. People either buy a book because it's been recommended or because its looks appealed to them enough to take it off the shelf. The cover has to convey the contents of the book or the strongest themes. It is what you show the retailers and

Looks are important. It's no good producing shoddy little books. Produce your cover so your book looks good enough to sit beside a novel by Jilly Cooper or the life story of Naomi Campbell.

the library suppliers; it can be reproduced on adverts or flyers. However, the more elaborate and colourful the cover, the more expensive it is to produce. This adds to the overall production costs and the publication price. You need to weigh up the cost against the extra sales which a well-designed, professionally produced cover is likely to generate. If you go to the expense of printing don't penny pinch here. However, sometimes the simple idea can produce striking results. If you work with a printer you know, they're usually helpful in coming up with cheap ways of achieving the effect you want. *(See Design Brief page 78.)*

Cover image

Your cover image must get across the essence of your text. It can be a photo, drawing or painting but it must be appropriate. Bad illustrations or badly reproduced photos can make your book look amateurish.

The title

Naming a book is like naming a baby - get it wrong and no-one is happy. Avoid in-jokes. Of course, you may find something really striking but as with design it's best to stick to the simple and straightforward. Make sure that the title conveys what the book is about. Try to avoid very long or complicated titles. One of the very early Yorkshire Art Circus books had the title *The Day The Russian Imperial Fleet Fired On The Hull Trawlermen 1904*. Needless to say there was little room on the cover for anything besides the words! Your title might be misleading or require a subtitle to get across the intended meaning. Try it out on some unsuspecting people. Ask them what your choice of title brings to mind.

Cover blurb

The blurb - the writing on the back cover - helps the buyer to make their decision. It usually gives a summary of the book's contents designed to hook the undecided

Perhaps titles always mean more to authors than to readers, who, as every writer knows, frequently forget or garble the names of books they claim to admire.
David Lodge, The Art Of Fiction

reader. Writing an effective blurb takes time and thought. Within the space of about two hundred words - or less - you have to advertise the benefits and features of your book, tell about the story without giving too much away while making it interesting enough for people to buy. Equally the blurb may consist of quotes from influential people. Look at other books. How do their blurbs come across?

Imprint - your publishing name

Your own imprint, ISBN numbers or bar codes are not essential if all you want to produce is one short print run book with a very limited local market, especially if your local book shops and newsagents are happy to stock the book as it is or if you just sell it face-to-face. If you plan to bring out a number of books it is worth setting up your press in a more professional way with your own imprint, ISBN numbers and bar codes.

You can operate your publishing venture under your own name or you can make up a separate name for your press. If your publishing programme is very focused, you may be able to come up with a name that gives readers an idea of what to expect. One small local press, Wakewalker Books, publishes books describing walks in the dales. But what's in a name? Some publishers, The Women's Press or Virago are two examples, indicate their programme through their name but the majority have names that are only loosely or not at all linked to their publishing programme. Bloomsbury, Minerva, Pan, Vintage, Faber & Faber, Hodder & Stoughton, Viking are all imprints that don't give away by their name what publishing programme to expect.

Check in the *Writers' & Artists' Yearbook* and also in *The Writer's Handbook* and in *Publishers In The UK And Their Addresses* that no one else is using your chosen imprint name. It is worth doing this at the outset so you avoid confusion and possibly conflict. You can set up a press without setting up a separate company but no matter how you have set up your press, remember that any income from your publishing venture is liable to tax.

Panther, Penguin, Puffin, Flamingo, Corgi, Ladybird, Bantam, Serpent's Tail, Black Swan, Phoenix, even Skunk, are all imprints but there are still quite a few animal names you can choose from when you name your press.

ISBN number

ISBNs, International Standard Book Numbers, are used by libraries and book sellers. This means your book is catalogued and can easily be located and ordered by quoting your ISBN. *(For address see page 74.)*

Your allocation of ISBN numbers is free. To get your allocation write to Whitakers and tell them how many titles per year you aim to publish. You will receive your free allocation of numbers consisting of a prefix which is like the numerical 'surname' of your press and the formula for working out your specific ISBN for each individual book. Yorkshire Art Circus numbers start with 1 898311; this is our prefix. Added to that are more numbers, these change for every book we publish. The formula which allows you to work out these changing numbers yourself is quite complicated. It is much easier and safer to buy a printout of your allocated numbers in full from Whitakers for a small fee.

Each individual title has to have its own ISBN number but if you are thinking of publishing a magazine where the title remains the same with the content changing from issue to issue, you will need an ISSN number instead.

Bar code

Like most other goods, commercially printed books carry a bar code. It allows electronic stock control and makes life easier for shops. When you order your bar code, you must state the size bar code you need and also quote the ISBN number of the book. *(To find out more, see page 74.)*

Spine

Giving the book a spine is an advantage. Not only does it look more professional and substantial but with the title and author's name on it, prospective buyers can find your book even when it's displayed on the shop shelf so that only the spine is visible.

When the letter with our ISBN allocation arrived I tried to work out the block of 50 numbers allocated to us. The instruction leaflet seemed straightforward but it was all a bit too mathematical for me so I sent off a cheque and got a full printout of our numbers.

Page design

Fonts

Designers and some publishers wax lyrical when they discuss fonts or typefaces. With little encouragement they reel off the names of their favourite typefaces: Garamond, Baskerville, Helevetica, Gill sans, Broadway, Palatino... the list goes on and is multiplied by the permutations of each typeface: light, medium, bold, condensed, italics... The typeface you choose makes all the difference. Buy four different newspapers and look at their front pages: What message do the typefaces convey?

You can give out very definite signals through the typefaces you use: this is a modern book, this is an authoritative book, this is an artist's book.

Parading the full menu of fonts before your reader may well detract from what you want to say. It's best to be disciplined: only the very brave or the very muddled mix more than two typefaces on a single page. Two typefaces, the possible use of bold or italic and the use of different point sizes will give you sufficient flexibility within a stylistic framework that can hold your text together and give it a strong identity.

For this book we chose Times New Roman as our typeface, with bold and italic and variations in point size. Other good typefaces for books are Garamond and Palatino. They are all serif faces, where the straight lines on the letters are softened by curved ends which make them easy on the eye.

Lay-out

For choice of lay-out and font look at some books you like or follow these basic rules:

• **Surround your letters by a generous amount of space**
If you can only afford a set number of pages and your choice is between squeezing it all on the page or cutting some text, cut!

The Baskerville type face is named after a Birmingham printer. When he died he was buried standing upright because he felt that a prostrate body could easily take the orientation favoured by some religion or other.

• The margins are important

A text that sits comfortably surrounded by paper is more pleasing to the eye and easier to read than a text that goes up to the edge of the paper and disappears in the gutter, the inner margin where the book is bound. There is also a limit on the line length our eyes are comfortable with; it's in the region of 11cms.

• Leading is important

> This is the gap between the lines. A smaller type size with generous leading is easier to read than a larger type size with little leading between the lines. For most books, 10pt on 13pt, ie point size (type size) 10 with leading size 13pt, is suitable for the body text.

Look at the difference. Here is the same text using point size 10, leading size 10:

> This is the gap between the lines. A smaller type size with generous leading is easier to read than a larger type size with little leading between the lines. For most books, 10pt on 13pt, ie point size (type size) 10 with leading size 13pt, is suitable for the body text.

Keep your style simple. A straightforward lay-out with one type face is not going to let you down.

Photographs/illustrations

If you want to reproduce illustrations or photographs check with a printer for the best techniques and the costs. Be sure that your illustrations or photographs work with your text and are of good quality; bad illustrations or photographs can make your book look amateurish.

If you include photographs this may determine the type of paper you print on and also your format; you should not need to turn the book to look at the image.

If you want to use other people's images or artwork check with them to make sure that you don't infringe on any copyright. Get their permission and sort any fees and acknowledgements. Some will want an acknowledgement next to each image, others will be happy with just a mention on the verso page.

A friend offered to do illustrations for my book. Unfortunately we hadn't realised that the only option in our printing budget was to use line drawings, so after I had taken everything to the printer's I had to ask my friend to re-do the illustrations. Next time I'll know that I need to check with the printer first.

Book construction

For the sequence of the first few pages look at some books and follow the pattern. Usually it goes

• title page

This gives the title, the author or editor, the publisher and the year of publication. There are no hard and fast rules. Different publishers tend to have variations on the theme.

• verso page

This is the back of the title page. The verso page gives the full details of the publisher, the ISBN number and classification. It acknowledges the cover design, photos and illustrations and printer. It can also carry the *moral right assertion* of the author.

• foreword/introduction/dedication

These are all optional and depend very much on the type of book you have in mind.

• page numbering

Page numbers help printers when they collate the book, they also help the reader, so unless there is a good reason against, use them. Look at other books for a model. By convention, left hand pages are even, right hand pages are odd numbers. Usually the preliminary pages before the main text don't carry page numbers but they are counted. Therefore the main text page numbering doesn't start at page one.

Book size

For one-offs you are in total control of book size. If you want to sell through shops you need to consider which formats will sit well on the shelves. Unless you are

For our first books with photographs we chose A4 vertical to make maximum use of the paper and to avoid off-cuts. Our readers felt these books didn't look like 'proper books' and bookshops found them difficult to place on the shelf: they were too floppy and also took up too much display space when placed face-on.

producing an artists' book, an A4 size book can easily look amateurish. It will flop about on the shop shelves and signal up 'magazine' rather than 'book'. Usually it is better to crop your A4 format to two thirds or four fifths. Look at books by other publishers. If you work with a printer they can advise you so your chosen dimensions don't waste paper. A5, either landscape (horizontal) or portrait (vertical) are good, tested standard sizes. If your book contains photos their dimensions will dictate whether you opt for a horizontal or vertical format.

Binding

You can have either a stapled or perfect bound cover. With a stapled cover the pages are folded and stapled through the centre fold into the cover; perfect bound means that there is no centre fold; the edges of the pages are glued into a spine.

Good-looking binding is essential to make your book look professional and handle well. Shoddy binding could mean that the book falls to pieces when it is opened up. For a one-off book or a very short print run, if you don't want to involve a professional binder, or if you are after something different, you may design some sort of folder rather than traditional binding, or maybe a beautiful box or a scroll.

I only produced one copy of my life story for my daughter. When it came to binding it I had it done professionally but it looked impersonal so I created a textile cover with embroidery and appliqué which makes my book a family heirloom.

The price on the cover

To arrive at a cover price you need to consider the cost of:
• Editing/proofing/typesetting
• Design
• Printing
• Marketing/distribution
• Review copies

• Editing/proofing/typesetting

Unless you find ways of getting these for free or you use your own time, consult the *Writers' & Artists' Yearbook*, the *Writer's Handbook* and the *Society of Freelance Editors and Proofreaders' Directory* to get an idea of the likely cost.

• Design

Ask around. Your printer may work with a designer; if you like their work give a clear brief and insist on a fixed fee. Generally speaking, the fewer design options you ask for, the smaller the fee to the designer. You could also try the local art college to see if students do this sort of work as part of their work experience, or to build up their portfolio. Expect to pay at least £50 for a cover design rough.

• Printing

The cost of a single copy - the unit cost - decreases the larger the print run. Don't be tempted though: if you opt for a large print run to keep the unit cost down, you may end up with too many books for too small a market. This means you won't generate enough money from the sales to cover the printing cost of the extra copies. You'll only benefit from a print run you can actually sell.

A prudent publisher will go for a high cover price and low print run. It is impossible to give a general idea of cost. There are too many variables: the cover, the number of pages, the dimensions, the paper quality and the number of photos.

• Marketing/distribution

Your advertising costs need to be considered here. If you distribute you must either cost postage and packing into the cover price, or charge them extra. Shops will expect you to pay for p&p to supply them and also for their returns.

If you go through shops or a distributor you will have to give a discount for every book sold. This is usually a percentage on the cover price. A distributor will take an additional discount on each copy placed with a shop or on each copy sold.

Some first-time publishers reckon to have made a profit but when you ask about their time and labour they have been working for nothing.

• **Review copies**

Your book needs to get talked and written about for people to want to buy it. As publisher you will have to stand the cost of sending out review copies for the media. Reviewers expect to receive free copies.

Fixing the price

Work out the unit cost

To find out the selling price, or cover price, of a single copy, start with calculating the unit cost:

Add up all your production costs, editing/proofing/typesetting, design and printing. Add overheads in as far as you need to take them into consideration. Obviously, if your book is a labour of love you may choose not to include your time and labour. Now divide your costs by the number of books produced. This gives you the unit cost to you, the producer, for one copy of your print run.

The commercial method

To work out the selling price a commercial publisher would multiply the unit cost by a factor of five: one for production, one for the author, one for profit and two for distribution. If all copies sell this will cover your costs *and* make a profit. If you are prepared to cut your profit margin and writer's fee you could multiply by a factor of three or even two if there are no distribution costs.

How would this work?

Let's say your production costs were £1650 for a print run of 500 copies.
Your unit cost would be £1650 divided by 500 = £3.30.
Multiply the unit cost by 5 to arrive at your cover price.
5 x £3.30 = would give you a cover price of £16.50.
Now take a deep breath and reconsider: how many people can you think of who would buy your book at this cover price?

The lure of the low unit cost has tempted many a self-publisher to over-produce. True, the unit cost will be down if you print 10,000 but you only benefit if you can actually sell your print run and you have enough cash to pay the printer's bill when it arrives.

What cover price can the market stand?

Let's start again. This time we will look at it from a different angle.

Let's say the costs come again to £1650 for a print run of 500.
From your print run deduct the number of review copies. Let's make that 50.
This leaves you with 450 books to sell. Of these, work out how many you will sell yourself at full cover price and how many will sell through book shops.

Let's assume you will sell 150 and you expect the shops to sell 300.
Now look in the shops. At what cover price do similar books sell?
Let's say, you find that £6 is the going rate.
Work out what your sales income could be if you charged £6 per book.
Your private, direct sales would bring in 150 x £6 = £900.
For sales through shops we'll assume a rather harsh shop discount of 50%, so shop sales would bring in 300 x £3 = £900.

Your maximum sales income would be £900 + £900 = £1800.

Congratulations, you are getting there, you have just managed to break even.

You can pay off your production costs of £1650, and you have £150 for postage.

There is no income here to cover your administration systems and you will have to be sure that you will sell your full print run just to break even.

You could now play through the figures on a cover price of £6.50, £7, and so on, up to the point where you feel that you have priced yourself out of the market.

If you have reached that point before you can recoup your production and other costs you need to modify the product to lower your production costs.

Big publishers make money because one book subsidises another. They can afford publicity material and promotion campaigns. Massive print runs bring down the costs significantly. As yet you are not in this league.

Realistically, on a small print run you won't recoup all your costs but you have a chance to become known as a writer. Go back to your reasons for publishing to determine whether and how you could compromise to stay within your budget.

On a small print run (less than 500 copies) we know we won't recoup all our costs. This is where it's important to go back to the reasons for publishing to determine whether and how to compromise.

Section Four

GO AHEAD

Production

Promotion

Quality control

Distribution

Dealing with outlets

Paperwork/administration

Set your own timetable

Now you have looked at all the options, you are in a stronger position to make your final decisions and settle on the text, design, budget and sales plan for your book. When you are totally happy with your choices, the time has come to get the presses rolling.

Production

Get your cover designed. Give your designer a clear brief specifying the size and the colour/s as well as the content of the book.

Once you're happy with the lay-out of the pages, typeset your text. Check that the lay-out is consistent. Do a final proof for spelling and punctuation. It is a good idea to get someone to read your text for you; you will be too familiar with it and you might no longer notice mistakes.

If you use photographs or illustrations indicate their position and size and whether they need cropping.

Punctuation matters. The Russian Revolution resulted from a decision by master printers not to pay their journeymen for commas!

Once you have chosen your printer you need to agree the exact job. Be clear about what material you give the printer to work from. Ideally your text should be on disk. Check that the software is compatible. Always include a hard copy - a printout of your text set out exactly as you want it - so that the printer can check against that. Do your preparation thoroughly and keep your instructions to the printer clear. Your next contact with the printer will be to proof the cover and the page lay-out. At this stage corrections are still possible but anything done in printer's time will cost you. Once the proofing at the printer's is done, the presses will start to roll. Any corrections afterwards will be very expensive, in fact you are probably looking at a reprint!

Promotion

While your book is being printed you need to finalise your promotion plan and start putting it into action.

Promotion is concerned with creating a demand and there is no philosopher's stone that tells you the best way to promote a book. The way you angle your promotion will depend on the book and the audience - the market which you have already researched before going into print.

Generally speaking you have two options, free promotion or paid advertising in a newspaper or magazine, or on a billboard. You must decide if the investment will generate enough sales to make a worthwhile return. With little money available for promotion and publicity, a newspaper advert is an expensive gamble. On the print runs we are envisaging we would recommend that you concentrate on free promotion. If you have to pay, this cost needs adding on to your cover price and not many people would buy a book *that* expensive by an unknown author.

Of course, if you have set up a subscription scheme you have already started your promotion.

You don't have to look any further than to politics to realise that all publicity - even bad publicity - can be turned into good publicity.

Whitakers

If you are going to sell your book through bookshops, get it in the British Library's Bibliographical Services Division system for Cataloguing In Publication (CIP). This will give the book a number and list the title in advance of publication, bridging the gap between publication date and the first reviews in the papers. The company J Whitaker supplies the CIP information to the British Library. Publishers need to give information of every new title on Blue Whitaker Book Information Forms, ideally well in advance of publication.

Word of mouth

The best promotion costs very little. Writing a book is an artistic achievement and people seem naturally interested. There is no reason why you can't start letting friends and relatives know as soon as the first draft is finished. Word of mouth is good free publicity.

Flyers/Advance Information

The flyer should persuade the reader to buy. It should be clear, crisp, concise, accurate and simple. Make it readable and intriguing. Set out benefits to the reader - what they will get out of this book - and factual details like the price and where the book can be ordered or bought. *(See Advance Information pages 82/83.)*

The flyer can be sent out near the publication date. Try and target your market as close as you can. If pensioners are the best audience, target old folks homes. If it's the young, target schools and colleges or youth clubs. For local interest books ask your local library to put up your flyer on their information board.

Advance information is a specialised flyer for the book trade. When you have your card covers printed for your book get the extra quantity you need printed on art paper. Then have your trade information printed inside with a summary of what the book is about, maybe a taster of the story and quotes from advance reviews if available. It makes an attractive flyer and adds relatively little to the print bill. It

When we put together one of our community books we make sure we get as many names and addresses of contributors as we can to invite them to the launch when the book is ready.

also allows the prospective buyer to see that they are getting a good, professionally-looking product and it reassures them that they are dealing with a reliable, well-organised publisher.

News Release

The publishing industry get a great deal of free coverage from the media, whether it's the Sunday supplements or the local radio station. Therefore, a news release should be sent to newspapers, radio stations, television programmes and anyone else in the media you think may be even vaguely interested. Scour the TV and radio listings for appropriate programmes, then mail your news release direct to named programmes, journalists or columns. Follow up the news release with a phone call to those papers or stations you think are most likely to take up your story. Remember, for an unknown author that usually means your local media.

Give information on the content of the book, but not a full synopsis or run-down of the plot. Newspapers are generally interested in newsworthy angles. A local human interest story is an easy scoop for local newspapers. Always ask the reporter to mention the price and your address so people can order direct. Unfortunately the editor may well take that information out of the copy because they see it as commercial advertising on the sly but it's worth a try. Talk radio shows have literary slots but radio brings few orders. *(See News Release page 81.)*

You need to give the following information **typed, double-line spaced, single-sided**:

• title, author's/editor's name

• ISBN, price, publication date, format - paperback or hardback -, publisher's name and address

• contact name and phone numbers where you can be reached

• brief (one page A4) outline of contents and, very important, anything newsworthy

When I write a news release I try to put myself in the shoes of the reporter or the editor. If I can give them lively, well-written, copy it makes their life easier and they are much more likely to use it.

- first paragraph to lead with something newsworthy

- your release may be chopped, so put the most important information first

- cover what? who? when? where? why?

- quote from named person

- date to stress that it's current news

Review Copies

It is false economy to stint on sending out review copies unless you are absolutely certain you can sell your full print run on word-of-mouth promotion alone. Review copies are paid for by the publisher.

As with the news release, review copies should be sent to named journalists and programmes. These should arrive on desks well in advance of the official publication date. This gives the media time to read the book and hopefully write the review.

Most literary editors of national newspapers like to receive their review copy five to six weeks before the publication date, whereas the regional or provincial papers can receive theirs a bit later. Periodical and less frequent magazines should be given longer. Radio and TV programmes that review similar titles should also be sent a copy. Local newspapers seldom take any notice unless there is a local angle, a connection between the author or the story and the locality.

A slip giving the publication date, and explaining that 'the book is sent for review, therefore no publicity or comment should appear before that date,' should be included. Your name and address should go on the inside cover of the book so that the media can contact you if they need more copies. Ask for a cutting from any review.

Both the news release and reviews are good ways of bridging the gap between the publication date and the first sales.

It's an uphill struggle. I sent out 40 review copies and managed to get two reviews. That's not bad going for an unknown publisher.

Author promotions

Book signings, readings and lectures or talks on the book topic can be a good way of selling. Start locally with shops, libraries and festivals. If there is a story behind the story, a magazine could do a feature on some aspect of the author's life or the book itself. Did the book take ten years, several relationships and a nervous breakdown to complete?

Launches

A launch is a good way to promote and sell. It doesn't have to cost the earth. As long as you get the right mix of people it can be enjoyable and productive. Pick the right venue. One of the most enjoyable launches we recall was of a local history book. The venue was a civic centre. At least half the numerous guests knew the author personally and everyone was interested in the subject of the book. Rehearsed readings gave a taster, everybody had a great time and the book sold very well.

Hype

A market can lose interest quickly so use hype to keep the title in the news. Hype is not just the prerogative of the Joan Collins's of this world but it comes their way more easily than ours or yours. If you have access to the media and are sufficiently extrovert, go for it. It is an excellent way of repeating the promotions campaign. One local author had his books returned to the limelight when one of his titles was cited in a custody case.

Awards

You obviously believe in your writing, so don't hide your light under a bushel. *The Writers' & Artists' Yearbook* has a comprehensive section on prizes and awards. Look at the requirements and decide which awards to enter for.

The launch was a real community event: everybody got their copy of the book and started leafing through for their own piece. The local MP made a speech, the rehearsed reading drew everyone into the collective achievement. It was the only book about this area and the whole community took pride in it.

The prizes vary, with £25,000 at the top end of the scale, but participation is everything. Have your news releases ready, there is publicity value even in just entering for an award, and definitely in getting shortlisted!

Your book is printed, what next?

The printer's van draws up and the boxes are unloaded. This is the moment you have been working for. You can't wait to see your creation, to open up the cover and see your writing transformed into a book.

Quality Control

This is a moment to savour but then you need to get back down to earth. Time for a quality check. A good, professional printer will have done a check but you need to be sure that you get your money's worth. Check:

- **the number of books delivered**

- **the quality of the binding:**
  Can you open the book out without pages coming loose?

- **the quality of the cover:**
  Is the colour constant?
  Are the edges trimmed evenly?
  Is the lamination smooth?

- **the quality of the production inside:**
  Is the inking even?
  Are the images well-produced?
  Is the binding straight?
  Are the pages in the correct order?
  Are the pages trimmed evenly and straight?

The book had been delivered on time. The launch was a great success, with a well-known speaker. The audience was queueing at the book stall. Suddenly a second queue formed. Those who had bought books had opened them for the author to sign and the books had shed pages. We had to collect all the books in, take everybody's address and mail out the next, perfect batch after playing hell with the printer.

Deposit copies for the British Library

Under the Copyrights Acts, you need to send off one copy each, within a month of publication, to

• the British Library

• the Bodleian Library, Oxford

• the Library of Cambridge University

• the Library of Trinity College, Dublin

• the National Library of Scotland

• the National Library of Wales (if requested).

The British Library copies must be sent direct, the others should be posted in one package, to the Agent for the Libraries. This is a legal requirement, so make sure you comply with it. *(The addresses for the deposit copies are under Contacts on page 74.)*

The only correspondence is a note to the British Library indicating the selling price. Your book will then appear, free of charge, in the *British National Bibliography*. This is a permanent record of British books in production which is scanned by acquisition librarians and larger booksellers both in the UK and overseas.

Copy for your local library

This is not a legal requirement but it is a nice way of sharing your story and getting it to local readers, especially if you have produced a very small number of copies. Your library could also act as a sales outlet. If your book has a strong local angle your library is likely to want to buy a few copies too. They usually have contact with other libraries in the region and might pass on information about your book.

It's quite a strange feeling to know that a copy of my book is sitting on the shelves of the British Library at Boston Spa, rubbing covers with the works of other writers; some famous, many unknown.

Distribution

Once your printer has delivered or you have collected your books you need to get them to the buyers. Basically there are two choices:

1- You find a distributor who will handle marketing and distribution for you. Typically the distributor will expect in the region of at least 55% of the cover price for each book placed with a sales outlet but they will handle marketing, repping of sales outlets and getting the orders to customers. If your market is scattered or national it is probably better to find a distributor. Find out from your Regional Arts Board if there's a distributor in your area or contact the Publisher's Association for their lists of warehouse and distribution services in the UK.

2- You do it! The question is how much time you can spend on this. If your book has a very localised market this is a viable option.

If you take on your own distribution you will have to deal with orders, queries in ordering, and customer complaints.

Dealing with outlets

Here is a list of tried and tested sales outlets. Some are more appropriate to small print runs and the cost of each of these needs working into your cover price.

The following all work well but reach limited numbers of potential buyers:

• **Personal touch**
works well for compact networks - family, friends, colleagues, clubs.

• **Subscription**
has the added bonus of helping your cash flow.

• **Launch**
can work a bit like subscription - you can have a special launch price to get people to buy sooner rather than later which is good for your cash flow.

I was lucky to find a distributor. This is the hardest job for a small press. They charge 55% on each book placed but if I wanted to rep all the regional book shops myself I would have a full time job on my hands.

• **Public reading/Book signing**

can work like a launch.

For distribution that goes beyond who you and your friends know, you could try:

• **Writers' festivals**

give you access to a specific readership but the competition is keen and you could waste a day with little to show in the way of sales.

• **Book fairs**

allow you to forge contacts within the industry and to sell your titles to retailers, wholesalers, library suppliers and academic suppliers. They may be too specialised for your needs and not within your budget.

• **Direct mail**

The flyer is best suited for this type of selling. Use your market research and mail out wisely. Once you get orders keep a list of who bought to use as a mailing list for your next book. Be sure your administration and despatch system is reliable. If you can ride piggy back on someone else's mail-out, that is a real bonus.

• **Book clubs**

Although roughly a quarter of people bought from book clubs, they only hold about 12% of the market value in the book industry. This is because the books they sell are usually cheaper; often they will have negotiated discounts of 60% or more with publishers.

Book clubs generate more sales because they have the resources to promote the books. They advertise in the *TV and Radio Times*, Sunday supplements and other periodicals like women's magazines, for example.

As a small publisher you may find book clubs appealing as they can generate more sales. Selling 1000 books through a book club is better than selling ten books through a book shop, regardless of market share.

As a small publisher we have not much choice but to go along with the conditions the big shops set. But there's hope. Signs are that more specialised book shops are finding their niche - and that gives small publishers a better chance.

• Book shops

Book shops in general are swamped by the output from the professional publishers, and a small book from a small press is unlikely to get much attention. However, many small publishers do sell to book shops. The market research suggests that they are worth approaching, particularly the big chains of book shops. They tend to order books through a central distribution computer and publishers frequently have to ask permission from the head office to approach a local branch.

When you work out how to market your book decide whether to saturate the local market by using additional outlets, like newsagents and supermarkets, or, if your book is suitable, sports centres or other venues, or whether you should place your book with book shops only but over a wider area.

Conditions

Shops will take books on a sale or return basis for an agreed period of time - 60 days is standard. They then settle up by returning unsold copies and by paying, on receipt of your invoice, for books sold. In the good old days shop discounts were around 33% of the cover price, now they are slowly moving up towards 50%. Distributors will take at least 55% but their cut usually includes the discount to shops.

Paperwork/administration

A book shop in Liverpool still owes me for five copies of my book. I don't think I'll get my money. Last time I came past, the shop was boarded up. My book obviously wasn't enough to keep them solvent.

Keep your systems simple.

You may receive a large number of small orders. You will also have to deal with unsold copies being returned and you must be able to credit the customer accordingly.

For all your outlets keep a record of where your books are and what the conditions are. Most outlets operate on sale or return. Remember that they take a discount.

They also expect you to pay for delivery and return costs for the books. The time lag between them receiving your invoice and paying can be three months. You really need a good system to record who has what, who needs contacting to establish sales and who needs chasing up because your invoice is overdue.

Delivery notes/Invoices/Credit notes

Delivery notes are despatched with your books and are followed up by invoices after the agreed sale or return period is up. You need to check how many books have been sold to invoice accordingly. Work out what suits you and negotiate with the shop if possible. 60 days is a reasonable sales period. Be prepared to follow the specific procedures required by a shop. If any books are returned after you have invoiced the shop you need to repay the shop and issue a credit note so the shop can clear their account with you. *(For forms see page 84.)*

We have put a sample delivery note and a sample invoice/credit note in the back of the book for you to use.

All your paperwork should include:

• your name or your trade name

• the issue date, also called tax point

• the name of the firm it's issued to

• title, quantity and price of book/s

• discount offered and any other special agreements

• amount due

Some companies wait for a monthly statement before paying. Avoid complications by writing, *No statement issued. Please pay on this invoice.*

You could try to cut down on paperwork and incorporate the delivery note and invoice into one document. Avoid misunderstandings by indicating whether the document is to be read as *Delivery Note* or *Invoice.*

With my first book I was totally unprepared. For me, holding the book in my hands was the happy ending. I hadn't really thought through what I'd do once I got the books but when I started to get cheques in the post with book orders I knew I needed to get myself set up properly.

Set your own timetable

Now we have to look at the sequence of events after you have made your decisions about the product and print run, publicity, marketing and distribution.

Work backwards from the launch or publication date and check that your time scales are realistic. This may be the point when you have to panic or speed up.

Launch/Publication date

Your launch/publication date can be arbitrary or it may link in with an event, maybe a festival at which your book could be launched. It gives a specific date to use in all promotional activities. Starting with this date work backwards to set deadlines. You need time for advertising, interviews, reviews - which can take several months - printing, typesetting, design and all the editing and rewriting. Allow at least a good six months after the completion of the final draft, less if you have a reliable printer and you are prepared to burn plenty of midnight oil.

Launch count-down

Your launch count-down for a professionally produced book with a print run of over 500 might look like this:

before the count-down	**decide on your readers/market**
	initial rough decision about your book
6 months before	**final draft ready**
	more detailed decision on book: design/shape/size/cover/print run
	determine your budget
	get printers/design quotations
	adjust book or adjust budget
	firm up market/subscription/share scheme

How long should it take? It's totally up to you. The idea of planning is to allow you to remain in control and achieve what you wanted to.

5 months before	**draw up promotion/marketing plan**
	get firm quotation from chosen printer
	finalise budget
	fix cover price
	design brief
	send off Whitaker's blue form
4 months before	**production**
	proof text/organise images if wanted
	lay out pages and typeset
	have cover designed: title/blurb/ISBN/bar code
	draft Advance Info (AI) text
3 months before	**printing**
	cover/AIs
	text to printer's
	page proof at printer's/cover proof at printer's
	promotion/marketing/distribution
	mail out news release/AIs
	set up marketing/sales administration
2 months before	**sell book**
	quality control
	legal deposit copies
	pre-launch promotion
	review copies to media
1 month before	follow-up news releases/AIs
3 weeks before	mail out launch invites
1 week before	copies to subscribers
LAUNCH	
after launch	deal with orders
	rep outlets

The commercial status and shelf life of the average book is similar to that of a tin of baked beans!

Section Five
Do-It-Yourself

If you want to produce your whole book yourself you need access to equipment and the know-how to use it.

Produce your text on a computer. This makes alterations to the text easier and allows you to desk top publish your text and, with the help of a laser printer, to produce high quality copy.

Unless you know a friendly printer who will trim your books for you keep to a standard format; like A5 vertical. If you opt for a stapled book there is a computer programme that will sort your pages and position them in the correct order.

You will need

• Personal Computer with desk top publishing software for the text
• laser printer for clean copy
• guillotine to trim the book (access to a friendly printer gives the neatest results)
• scanner if you intend to scan in photos
• colour printer for the cover
• long-arm stapler if you go for a stapled cover
• photocopier

How to bind your book

Traditional binding
There are book binding courses available at art colleges. The alternative is to do everything else yourself but use a professional book binder.

Heat seal binding
A heat seal binder with blank covers costs in the region of £200. See if you can locate one at your local resource centre. The drawback is, the covers only take a

When the poet William Morris founded Kelmscott Press in 1890 he was able to create beautiful books because he had taught himself all the skills needed.

specific number of pages, they are blank and you can't overprint. You could print off dust covers on a colour printer. This only works if your cover is small enough for a dust cover out of an A4 sheet which is the biggest size most ink jet printers can handle. One alternative would be to produce and print the cover on an ink jet printer, then copy it enlarged on a colour photocopier.

DIY binding

1. Staple the sheets in groups of twenty, then glue the groups together down the stapled edge.

2. Take a large piece of paper and wrap it around the manuscript (forming an inside cover), gluing it to the spine. You can write any dedication or copyright claim on this.

3. Take card and score two lines down the centre, making sure they are the width of the spine apart. The card should now fold neatly around the manuscript as the outside cover.

4. Glue the centre of the card to the spine.

5. When dry, stencil the lettering to the front of the book. If you enjoy painting, collage or embroidery you could create your own special cover image.

Other formats

Your publication does not have to be in book form. You could keep it in a beautiful container, you could keep it as a scroll. You may have written your story as individual pieces that fit onto an A4 sheet each. One of the attractions of this type of publication would be that it is not kept in a rigid order but that it can be read in a number of sequences.

There is no such thing as a moral or immoral book. Books are well written, or badly written.
Oscar Wilde, 1854-1900

Section Six

WRITING

Reasons to write your story

Golden rules

Content

Putting pen to paper

Form

Structure

Editing

Reasons to write your story

Why do we write? It's a common place that everybody has at least one book in them, and writing clearly satisfies a deep human need for self-expression. Writing needs little more than a pen and paper to get started so it is immediate and accessible. Telling our stories is a universally popular activity. Some people write for themselves, others for a wider audience. It may be that we need to make sense of what has happened in our lives, it may be that we want to leave a record either for our family and friends or for the world at large.

Every writer has different but valid reasons for writing. There are no right or wrong reasons but it is useful though to understand why you write because this will affect what you do next with your writing.

• What do you want to get out of writing?
• Do you write purely for yourself, or do you want others to read it?

By telling your story, the knowledge you have will become understanding. And that - knowledge becoming understanding - is better than anything there is to feel.
Tom Spanbauer,
The Man Who Fell In Love
With The Moon

- What is it you want to say?
- Do you wish to entertain, to record, to inform, to teach, to get rich and famous?
- Who do you intend to read it? Family and friends? Complete strangers?

Honesty is vital here. Your personal answers will begin to point to the most appropriate form of publication for your writing. The nice thing is, this doesn't have to stop you from publishing; on the contrary, it helps find the best publishing solution for *you*.

If at this point you are saying, I haven't even started yet and nothing could be further from my mind than working out what to do with the finished text, think again. Unless you are really just writing for yourself you need to be aware of your readers. Writing and publishing are two interlinked processes. When you talk to someone that person is there and their reactions are immediate. You have to find a way to touch your reader. When you write a story your reader may be miles, or centuries, away from you. If you want your story to speak to others you have to have a reader in mind as you are writing. There is no one recipe for the right blend of words that will draw and hold readers to your story - just look at the wealth of different writing around you. That is the joy of writing but also the risk. Here is a list of ingredients that will help your writing to be interesting; how you mix them together is up to you and makes your writing unique so that it conveys your very own story in your very own way.

Golden rules

The writing process isn't all that clean-cut; lots of decisions are interdependent and need to be made virtually at the beginning when you start writing your text. Some considerations apply universally to any type of writing, whether it's largely factual or purely fictitious.

There are a few golden rules and like all good rules, the art is in knowing when to apply them and when to ignore them.

The craft of writing requires control over language and the ability to tell a gripping tale. If it is worth doing it is worth doing well!

• Always keep the readers in mind

Your readers will be an unpredictable lot. They come to your text with their own background and experience and this will colour how they read your words. They assume things you don't want them to and they all interpret words and phrases differently. They need to become your partners across time and space to recreate your text in their reading. You have to invite them into your writing but you also need to give them space to interpret your words and to read between the lines.

• Show, don't tell

Make a connection with the reader. Don't spoon-feed the reader but give them an active part to play in the act of reading. Instead of telling the reader that Aggie and Billy don't get on, this scene illustrates their feelings through their actions. This way the reader is given the opportunity to work out for themselves what the relationship is.

On entering the house she began putting her shopping away and Bill Buckingham put on the kettle. 'I'll have my china cup.' She nodded towards the cup which stood upside down on a saucer next to Bill's enormous thick pint pot.

'Aw, thee and tha fancy ways.'

'I can't help the way I'm made, William.'

'Can't help what! Why, tha wasn't brought up, tha was dragged up. Thee father never did a day's work in his life. House full o' kids. I knew thee when tha was ragged arsed at school.'

Aggie pulled her lips into a straight line; she didn't like him to bring up her past. She had tried to get away from it. That's really why she had married Bill Buckingham. He was known as a good worker who never missed a shift and brought home a good pay packet. Not as she ever knew what he earned but then neither did any other woman in Denaby Main.

Evelyn Haythorne, In Our Backs

As you are reading these words, you are taking part in one of the wonders of the natural world. For you and I belong to a species with a remarkable ability: we can shape events in each other's brains with exquisite precision...That ability is language...The ability comes so naturally that we are apt to forget what a miracle it is.
Steven Pinker,
The Language Instinct

• Write in the first person

You are closer to the reader if you use *I* or *we*, than if you remain *he* or *she*:

'Don't make me go away. Let me stay here!' I begged. But he paid no heed and carried me into the kitchen where he took out a small bottle of whisky from his pocket and, pouring some into a cup, offered it to me.

'I can't take intoxicating liquor!' the Rechabite in me mumbled. It sounded so silly that I had to fight the compulsion to laugh for I knew that it would not be laughter that came from my throat but the screams which I could feel building up inside me.

Evelyn Haythorne, On Earth To Make The Numbers Up

• Dramatise scenes so they become more immediate

This makes for lively reading and again is a way to include the reader by allowing them to follow the story as it unfolds.

'It seems very small,' I said the pathologist.

'Yes, it is quite small. Normally we wouldn't expect to find such a small heart in someone suffering from a heart condition.'

'Why?' I questioned, wondering if he was suggesting that I hadn't really needed a transplant.

'Well, the stress on the heart often means it becomes enlarged.'

'Oh...' I said, not knowing what else to say. 'Where's the hole?'

He touched it again and it fell into four pieces. 'We cut it into quarters to examine it,' he explained, seeing my shocked face. 'Here's the septal defect,' he said, poking his finger through the flesh.

The four pieces of my heart lay on the stainless steel table, slightly tinged with blue and very ordinary. I felt totally unmoved, this was just a quartered muscle.

Jo Hatton, Future Conditional - My Heart/Lung Transplant

The German word for art, Kunst, *comes from the same root as the word for being able to,* können.

• Be specific and concrete, give precise details of names and places

This creates a sense of location and gives the reader points of reference outside the story.

I was out of the car, and I rushed up to the man. I didn't wait, I was straight in, a bit unusual when you think of it. I'm usually cautious. 'Excuse me,' I said, 'but what do they call you?'

'Nay lad,' he said - he'd got that sort of twang that they have out there, 'nay lad what do they call you?'

'They call me Lofthouse.'

Well, his face changed. 'That's my name too!'

'You look like my dad.'

I was standing there not knowing what to do. It was his turn to speak. 'Where do you come from lad?' he said.

'Pontefract.'

'I'm sure you'll be some relation. I'd a brother but he came from Featherstone.'

'No,' I said, 'I live in Pontefract now but my folks come from Featherstone.'

'Well, you'll be Ernie's lad!'

Sarah had come over by this time and was standing listening. 'I'm your Uncle Art. Come inside and meet your dad's sister, your Aunt Emma. Mind, she'll say she's seen you on that music box in the corner.'

Geoff Lofthouse, A Very Miner MP

'Grammatical' is not necessarily 'meaningful'; provided your writing can be understood, the accurate reflection of what you want to express is more important than rules of grammar.

• Write from the viewpoint of 'you' at different ages rather than filtering everything through your old and wise self

'Where's God come from?' one of the Thompson lads asked.

'I don't know. Heaven I suppose.'

'He doesn't, my mam says he's all around us and this isn't heaven is it? Heaven's up there,' piped in our Herbert.

'If heaven's up there, and God's in it, how come he doesn't fall out onto us?' asked our Barry.

'He has a big chair and he sits in it all day listening to prayers and people asking for things. That's why he doesn't fall on us, clever clogs.' Herbert threw back his answer with false assurance.

'Did he mek chair his self or did angels help him?'

'I don't know. God doesn't tell you everything, you know, he leaves you to find out things from other people.'

Rosie jumped in, 'Yes, like me, and where babies come from.' She beamed.

Walt Palmer, Mother's Ruin

• Bring your beliefs and passions to life through stories rather than forcing them on your readers as sermons

When I was a child I was treat as child. I was told many lies, like all children are told lies... For instance, when I small, and the wind whistle and howl round the house where I live, and I tremble in my shirt for fear, mother used to say: 'Slave Master coming! You be good boy or Slave Master take you!' *It were not true, noise was the wind whistling and my mother tell me lie to* control *me. Children don't know much and for this reason they can be control by untrue stories.*

At school, when I did go to school, teacher tell stories from Bible. Only stories ever told me as a kid were from Bible. My mother don't tell me stories, and my father work so hard I don't see him long enough for stories. Father ask me if I done my work with the animals; is everything fine concerning cultivation of field?

With my eyes and my hands I learn about things around me, how to control horse or catch wild animal or grow plant. With my ears I learn stories told by teacher.... As a kid I believe this, I told *to believe, I* made *to believe. As I get older I start to ask question.*

Alfred Williams, To Live It Is To Know It

Persons attempting to find a motive in this narrative will be prosecuted; persons attempting to find a moral in it will be banished; persons attempting to find a plot in it will be shot.
Mark Twain, 1835-1910

• **Be honest with your readers**

Be clear about the areas you want to keep from them. There is nothing wrong with holding back - you are in control of your life story - but don't drop dark hints of superior knowledge, nobody likes to be led on or teased.

• **Treat your readers with respect**

If you invite someone to share your life story and you expect them to spend time reading it you need to have put in time and effort preparing it. Usually this means working on your story through several drafts.

Content

Often when people write their life story they feel they must tell all, that omission would be dishonest or leave their life story incomplete. This isn't the case.

At the point where you decide about publication you need to consider carefully how open you are: how far are you prepared to bare all; how sensitive will you be of the feelings of the people you write about? There is no right or wrong; the important thing is to be aware of your choices and the possible consequences.

If you are convinced that nothing can be left out, write it. If nothing else, it will give you extensive raw material for your life story. It is very likely that, as you read it, you will become aware of contentious or boring passages which you will want to change or edit out. If you are fundamentally troubled by 'lying through omission', it's worth considering that our whole life is an editing process. Our memory is naturally quite selective.

But which facts?' Arthur asked him. 'Which facts do we print, Ishmael?'
David Guterson, Snow Falling On Cedars

Life is an excellent resource. Sometimes it's stranger than fiction. But how do you remember everything that happened? The answer is, you don't. Freud once commented that everybody's life was incomplete - there are things we don't remember and there are things we choose to forget. The things we do remember are distorted and segmented. Remember that and work positively with the natural editing process that keeps most of us sane most of the time. Accept it, use it to shape your story. Don't worry about leaving things out.

So how do you go about remembering? Well, certainly relatives, friends, work colleagues could all help revive incidents long since forgotten. Old photographs may help, as will letters, diaries or journals, job applications, certificates - anything that stimulates your memory. Try to build up an archive to support the archive in your mind.

Putting pen to paper

How do you start writing? The answer here is really that simple: just put pen to paper and begin anywhere! There is no point agonising. If nothing else comes to mind, start with 'I was born on...in...to....' Remember, this is just the starting point for your writing, not for your structure. Before you get to that you need to have done quite a bit of writing. In order to build up your material, you could use the salami tactic: Imagine your life sliced up into small, manageable bites: birth, first memories, first day at school... Keep slicing at the salami until it's all there on the platter. Then you can start arranging it into a pattern or display to suit you. Or try the Swiss cheese method: imagine the solid slab of cheese which needs holes boring into it. Your writing could extract probes of first love, friends, talents, triumphs, failures and hopes.

The working title

Go for something short and to the point. Test your title by trying it on willing friends. Ask them to give you a description of the book your title suggests. A publisher may still want to change your title to promote your book, or because it has already been used.

Sitting in his underwear on the edge of his bed he wanted to write something about the watch, but on the empty page could manage only a stiff, insufficient sentence...
Annie E Proulx, Postcards

Form

Besides writing a fairly straightforward prose autobiography there are other ways of approaching your life story. You might write a series of poems or short stories, or combine different types of writing. Experiment until you come up with a format that you feel comfortable with and that inspires and supports your writing.

Peter Hellings wrote his life experience as a series of sonnets. He worked as an English teacher in an inner city Birmingham School:

Real Thirst

Classes creep in,
                              ragged reluctant brooks
babbling between desks to find a place
where empty talk can fill the empty space
of casual concentration on closed books.

No glittering streams replenish this dull lake
where undercurrents of disturbance rise,
visible on the surface,
                              like the skies
professional sailors watch for storms to break.

The climates of our time evade control:
what can we do for a fermenting lake
or stagnant reservoir where few can drink?

I watch the bubbles on this sea of ink:
cannot we find ways for each kid to slake
real thirst at a clear natural waterhole?

Peter Hellings, A Form Of Words, An Autobiography In Verse

All story telling and writing is a re-working of the few basic plots and the human experience we all share.

Structure

Do you want to cover the whole of your life, or just childhood and growing up? How will the people in your story react if they read your story? Could people feel hurt? How will you cope with their reactions? How much will you make this a story of your most private thoughts and experiences or a story linking you into the history of your time, maybe a story dealing mainly with you at work or you and your politics, you and your family?

Once you know which parts of your life story you will write about you also need to start thinking about the overall structure. This means putting your writing into the sort of order which turns it from a rag bag collection of reminiscences into something complete and whole. Think of your structure as a house: which are the load-bearing parts, which the doorways leading from one part to another, which are the rooms you will lead the reader to or through? Where will you start - from the porch for a systematic tour? - or from your favourite spot? Will you give each room the same significance or will you hurry through some rooms while lingering in others?

Of course, writing in chronological order provides a sound structure but maybe that's too predictable. It could also mean that your structure plods along in a straight line of years and fails to highlight the really important events or themes of your life. You could structure your life story through

• **significant dates from your life:**

birthday, first day at school, school leaving, first date,...
or childhood, school days, work, retirement,...

or

• *important relationships*:

me and my parents,
me and my siblings,
me and my partner/s,

It is impossible to read any of his stories from the last line to the first without experiencing a definite sensation of going backward. This seems to me to prove that the stories were written and did not just suddenly materialise.
James Thurber,
The Thurber Carnival

me and my children,
me and my friends
me and my colleagues
or

• *forces you think shaped your life:*

faith, politics, convictions, love, hatred, envy, adversity, illness...

Once you get used to writing regularly you can start looking at your writing critically. Most writers produce several drafts until they're happy with their story. Try out different approaches until you're happy with the result. A good structure will support your story and help it along. Remember, your story could start anywhere. 'The very beginning' may well be the very best place to start to write your first draft but when it comes to your final draft the beginning of your story could be anywhere: the time of your conception or birth, a central, happy or traumatic event that shaped the rest of your life, a look back on your life starting with you as you are now. Your opening lines will probably be written towards the end of the whole process because you need to have a clear idea of your structure. It is crucial to find a way to captivate your readers and draw them in.

This is a strong opening, allowing us straight in and enticing us to find out more:

'Aggie, bring thee body up here and stop yacking.'

'Coming William.'

'Well, come on now or does tha want me to fetch yer?'

'Don't shout William. I'm just talking to the lady.'

'Well, fetch thee fat arse up here and let the lady get sommatt done.'

'Oh, do excuse me. William doesn't like me to be out of the house for ten minutes when he's at home.' She turned and with a set smile on her face scurried towards her husband.

Evelyn Haythorne, In Our Backs

Time is the medium of the narrative, the same as it is the medium of life.
Thomas Mann, 1875-1955

This opening also demonstrates a good way to handle dialect. There is much disagreement about how to represent dialect faithfully in writing. Devising your own spelling can create a real barrier for the reader. The best solution is to remain as close as you can to standard spelling. You can then still get across the rhythm of the dialect and introduce dialect words but without losing the reader's attention.

Editing

There's a huge sigh of relief as you cross the last *t* and dot the page for your last full stop. Now for the hard bit. Take a holiday of at least two months from the manuscript, because the next time you look at it you're going to have to be objective, critical and downright mean. You will have to edit and refine every page. Now is not the time for literary vanity, the ego must go back in the box.

Start with the length. If you cut anything will the story still make sense? If yes, get out the red pen. A good rule of thumb is to aim to cut by at least one third.

Time for Miss Marples: look for inconsistencies. Make sure your dates add up, your characters are consistent. This is especially important if you have fictionalised your story by giving people and places different names.

Next, look out for your favourite phrases. They will be dotted through the text liberally and repetitively. Unless you can justify them as a stylistic device essential to your writing get rid of them - you are better off without them.

Go back to the structure. Is the emphasis where you want it? Do you find that important bits have been left out or underwritten?

Does the story flow as you wanted it to? Does the dialogue sound convincing? One good way of testing is by reading out aloud.

Get others to read your writing. Even after a break you are too close, you need someone to look in from the outside. Family or friends may also be too close to

In composing, as a general rule, run your pen through every other word you have written; you have no idea what vigour it will give your style.
Sydney Smith, 1771-1845

comment honestly. You need people with no direct stake in your writing. A local writers group could give you some feedback. Hopefully it will not only be honest but also constructive in its criticism so that you can react to it in a practical way.

What's more, writers groups offer ideal opportunities for you to get involved with the business of writing. A mistake many writers make is to shut themselves away. Workshops or groups are often in touch with writing festivals or publishing projects. They hold readings where you can introduce your work to a wider audience and they allow you to make contact with people in the industry.

That evening there was a big get together in the cellar. A student social, they culled it. Everyone was singing, drinking, reciting poetry, giving bits of plays... I decided to give a few of my poems an airing. I was pretty drunk.

Next morning I daren't go down. 'Let's hope,' I thought, 'that no-one recognises me as the boring sod who got up and read her poetry to a captive audience.'

This bloke came up. 'Are you the girl who gave that poetry reading last night?'

'Yes,' I said, 'I think I'd had too much to drink.'

'It was good,' he said. 'I hope to hear more of you.'

'He's pulling my leg,' I thought but he wasn't.

Others came too. Brian Sefton asked me if I'd come to the English class and read.

That night I went into the grounds. As I walked through the trees I started to cry. I cried for those wasted years. I cried because it had taken me thirty-three years to realise that I was an individual. I cried for the women who couldn't see further than the hoover and the duster... I cried till I ached. Not just for myself but for the thousands of women like me who had never had a chance to breathe.

'Let each man's hope be in himself.' It took me a long time to understand what my dad meant, but now I understand I'll pass the message on to my daughter.

'Let each woman's hope be in herself.'

Julia Young, Getting Ideas

Publish and be damned.
Arthur, Duke of Wellington,
1769-1852

Section Seven

USEFUL INFORMATION

Glossary of Publishing Terms

Here is a vaguely alphabetical list of terms used in the text and also the main terms a printer might use. If in doubt, ask your friendly printer!

A4/A5

A4 and A5 are common paper sizes used for office stationery. SRA2 is a printer's sheet size. They come in horizontal (or landscape) and vertical (or portrait).
A4: 210mm x 297mm
A5: 148mm x 210mm
SRA2: 450mm x 640mm

Bar code

Your bar code is based on the ISBN number of your book. Your bar code allows electronic stock control and makes life easier for shops.

Binding

Let your printer know which binding you choose, it affects the page lay-out for printing.

> **stapled/stitch-sewn/saddle-stitched:** *The pages are stapled along the spine, usually along a centrefold. You could do this yourself with a long-arm stapler. This binding doesn't give you a spine with space for a title; your publication will look like a pamphlet rather than a book.*

> **perfect bound:** *The pages are glued into a spine and, depending on the width of the spine, there is room for a title along the spine.*

> **burst bound:** *This is similar to perfect bound but the pages are first section sewn to bind them more securely, this is recommended on thick or large books.*

Camera ready copy
This is copy ready for making the film and plates for printing.

Collating
This means gathering the folded, printed sections ready for binding.

Colour
Each colour means a separate run through the presses, this adds to the cost, so colour tends to be used on the cover only, the inside text is black or one dark colour throughout.

> **full-colour:** *also known as* four colour process, *this allows the printer to create a full range of colours out of the process colours magenta, yellow, cyan plus black.*

> **two-colour/three-colour/four-colour:** *This process is a job for your designer or printer; it involves colour separation. It is cheaper than full-colour. The range of colour is limited but a clever design can make an extra colour go a long way.*

Design rough
This gives the printer the idea for the cover, with the cover image, the specifications for the lettering and the positioning of the artwork on the cover.

Desk top publish (dtp)
DTP is a means of creating the final lay-out and typesetting by computer.

Disk
Before you do your own typesetting on a computer check with your printer to make sure their equipment can read your disk or that there is a way of converting your disk.

DocuTech
This is a fairly new reproduction process allowing small 'print runs' to be produced more cheaply than with conventional printing.

End paper
This is the plain, coloured paper between the binding and the printed pages.

Finishing

This describes the process of laminating, binding and trimming.
Small printers sometimes subcontract finishing which is a part of the book production process. This means that laminating, binding and trimming are done elsewhere. If a fault occurs in these areas do not negotiate directly with the subcontractor; your contract is with the printer and it is their job to deliver quality.

Gutter

This is the inner margin. When you design the page lay-out make sure you take into account that your book won't open flat; you have to leave a bigger inner margin to compensate for the binding.

Hard copy

This is a computer printout of your text. Always enclose a hard copy with your disk. This way, if there is a variance between your copy and the printer's version they can correct it to make sure that they reproduce your lay-out.

Heat seal

This is a type of perfect binding using ready-made covers, usually plain. The heat seal covers have glue on the inside of the spine. To bind you use a special heat seal binder which heats the glue and sets the pages into the bed of glue.

Imposition of pages

This is the way the pages are laid out on the printer's sheet to fold into sections for collating and binding. The imposition is determined by the size book you want to produce. Books are usually printed on SRA2 size sheets (450mm x 640mm). You can print 8 pages A5 onto this format. Since each sheet is printed double-sided, one sheet will give you 16 pages. The printed sheets are then folded, collated and gathered for binding.

ISBN

International Standard Book Numbers are used for books and catalogued centrally through Whitakers. Libraries/book sellers can locate a book by its ISBN number. The number consists of a publisher's prefix and additional numbers identifying a specific title.

ISSN
International Standard Serial Numbers function like ISBNs for periodicals and magazines where the title remains the same for a series of issues.

Justification
This means giving your text straight edges by making all the lines exactly the same length rather than leaving the edge ragged.

Laminate
This is the protective layer put on the cover after printing; you can choose between gloss or matt, or even a combination. You can also use spot UV varnish which is high gloss. Without lamination a cover gets to look grubby very quickly.

Laser printer
These printers are used with a personal computer (PC). Whereas the older type daisy wheel printer or an ink jet printer will show up the little dots that compose each letter, a laser printer will produce much smoother outlines for the individual letters and therefore better quality copy. Sometimes, eg for DocuTech, a printer will be able to use laser hard copy to print from.

Leading
This is the space between lines of print. Generous leading is more important than big point size to make your text easy to read.

Pagination/page numbering
Left-hand pages are even, right-hand pages odd.

Paper formats
Any size is possible but at a price. Look in book shops to see which formats are common and check with your printer for a format that uses paper economically. Printers usually work from an SRA2 sheet of paper. Remember, you pay for all the paper used on your book, including the off-cuts. A4 is not a very satisfactory book size. 2/3 A4 or 4/5 A4 are more pleasing to the eye and less floppy on the shelf. A5 works well both vertically and horizontally.

Paper orientation

    landscape (horizontal) or portrait (vertical): *Your choice depends on whether you want to reproduce photos, and what their orientation is.*

Paper weight/samples

The weight and type of paper depend on whether you want to reproduce photos but also on the look and feel you want to create. Most books use paper from 80 gsm to 130 gsm for inside. For the cover use card, 230 gsm (315 micron) or thereabouts is normal. Paper comes in different finishes, Gloss Art, Matt Art, Velvet. Consult your printer on cost and suitability. Always ask to see samples, papers of the same weight can feel very differently.

Paper colour

If you want to print on off-white or a colour talk to your printer. There may be extra cost and it may change the reproduction of photographs or illustrations.

Photographs

For the inside of your book black and white is considerably cheaper than colour. Your printer can work from transparencies or actual photos.

Plate

The final text is imposed onto film, then onto a plate which is inked up for printing. Plates can be metal or photopolymer; for very short runs a printer may use paper plates. For these good copy is essential.

Preliminary pages

They usually come in this order:

title page
verso page (This is the reverse of the cover page; it usually contains the technical details.)
dedication (optional)
contents (optional)
foreword (optional)
introduction (optional)

Proofs

page lay-out proofs: *This is an essential part of your quality control because it is your last opportunity before printing to check that your text is laid out as in the master copy you gave the printer to work from and that the lay-out hasn't slipped. At this stage you also need to make sure that the photographs or illustrations have been placed and captioned correctly and that they haven't been inverted.*

cromalin proofs: *These are used in four colour work to check the cover. The colours are approximate.*

Spine

Only perfect or burst bound books have a spine that can be printed on. The advantage is that your book title can be read on the shelf. Staple-sewn books look more like a pamphlet.

Typeface/Font

This is the style of lettering. The shape of the letters in a newspaper or book varies. The style of a letter is called typeface or font. Each font has variations: the type face can be normal, bold or italics. Easy to read faces for your text are Times New Roman, Garamond, Palatino. You may want to use a different font for your headings, Arial or Helvetica, or you could have your headings in bold.

Type size/point size (pt)

This measures the size of the letters. For most books, between 9pt and 12pt are good sizes.

Run-on

When you ask printers for a quotation, ask for the number you want - 500 or 1000 - plus a run-on of 100. These two figures will allow you to calculate rough printing costs if you change your eventual print run.

Run-on on pages

When you ask for the printer's quotation you may not know the exact number of pages of your book. Guess the most likely number and ask for a run-on on pages in multiples of four.

Sale or return
Most outlets will only take your book if they can return the unsold copies within a specified time and only pay for copies sold.

Software
Make sure your computer software is compatible with the printer's or can be converted into something compatible.

Widows and orphans
These are incomplete lines of text at the top or bottom of the page. Wherever possible avoid them by re-writing the copy to create full lines.

Further Reading

John Singleton & Mary Lockhurst (ed), *The Creative Writing Handbook - Techniques For New Writers*, Macmillan 1996

Clare Boylan (ed), *The Agony And The Ego,* Penguin Books 1993

David Lodge, *The Art Of Fiction*, Penguin Books 1992

Peter Finch*, How To Publish Yourself,* Allison & Busby 1991

*The Print Production Handbook***,** Macdonald & Co (a good all-round book on production/ printing but very little on desk top publishing and computer use in publishing)

Charles Foster, *Editing, Design And Book Production*, Journeyman 1993

Ros Jay, *Marketing Your Small Business*, Hodder & Stoughton 1996

Moi Ali, *The DIY Guide To Marketing* Directory of Social Change 1996

Contacts

Legal Deposits:

British Library, Copyright Receipt Office, 2 Sheraton Street, London, W1V 4BH

Agent For Libraries, 100 Euston Road, London, NW1 2HQ

ISBN:

J Whitaker and Sons, 12 Dyott Street, London, WC1A 1DF
(0171 4206008)

ISSN:

The ISSN UK Centre, The British Library, Boston Spa, Wetherby, LS23 7BY
(01937 546959)

Bar Code:

Find out what sizes of bar code are available so you can put the dimensions in your design brief. Bar codes are supplied by specialist suppliers. Check your *Yellow Pages* or trade directories under *Barcoding, Label Makers* or *Marking & Identification Services.*

Trade manuals:

The first two are invaluable for anybody considering getting into publishing. They have lists of publishers, agents and how-to information useful for authors and publishers.

Writers' & Artists' Yearbook
A & C Black, 35 Bedford Row, London, WC1R 4JH

Writer's Handbook
Macmillan, 25 Eccleston Place, London SW1W 9NF

Publishers In The UK And Their Addresses
J Whitaker and Sons, 12 Dyott Street, London, WC1A 1DF

The Bookseller, 12 Dyott Street, London, WC1A IDF
(the trade magazine with information on trends and developments, available at your local library)

Society of Freelance Editors and Proofreaders' Directory, 38 Rochester Road,
London, NW1 9JJ

Publishers in the UK and their Addresses, J Whitaker and Sons, 12 Dyott Street,
London, WC1A 1DF

Small Press Group , Small Press Centre, Tottenham Campus, White Hart Lane, Tottenham,
London, N17 8HR

Small Presses and Little Magazines in the UK and Ireland, Oriel, The Friary,
Cardiff, CF1 4AA

Radical Bookseller, 265 Seven Sisters Road, London, N4 2DE

Irish Publishing Record, The Library, University College, Belfield, Dublin 4, Ireland

Irish Booklore, Dept of Library and Information Studies, Queens University,

Belfast, Northern Ireland, BT7 1NN

Llais Lyfrau / Book News, Welsh Books Council, Castell Brychan, Aberystwyth, Wales

Books in Scotland, The Ramsay Head Press, 15 Gloucester Place, Edinburgh, EH3 6EE

Warehouse and Distribution Services

Comprehensive lists of warehouse and distribution services in the UK are available from:

The Publisher's Association, 19 Bedford Square, London, WC1B 3HT (0171 580 6321)

There are distributors for small press publications:

Password, New Mount Street, Manchester, M4 4DE
Turnaround, Unit 3, Olympia Trading Estate, Coburg Road, Wood Green, London N22 6TZ

UK Book Shops

A full list of UK book shops is available from:

Booksellers Association Annual List of Members
154 Buckingham Palace Road, London, SW1W 9TZ (0171 730 8214)

Radical Book Shops Guide (Federation of Radical Book shops)
c/o Houseman's Book Shop, 5 Caledonian Road, Kings Cross, London, N1 9DX.

Writing Courses

Adult Education courses
Information is available from local authority education departments or the WEA.

Open College of the Arts
Houndhill, Worsbrough, Barnsley, S70 6TU (01226 730495)
The OCA offers distance learning creative writing and life story writing courses, accredited by the University of Glamorgan.

Arvon Foundation
Lumb Bank, Hepton Stall, Hebden Bridge, HX7 6DF (01422 843714)
The Arvon Foundation offers a variety of short residential writing courses at all levels for people with a genuine interest in writing at its centres at Lumb Bank, Moniack Mhor, Scotland and Totleigh Barton, Devon.

Writers' Groups

Ask at your local library or college for information on writers groups in your area.

Manuscript Reading Service

Yorkshire Art Circus, School Lane, Glasshoughton, Castleford, WF10 4QH (01977 550401)
Please send self-addressed, stamped envelope for our fact sheet.

Book Production Courses

Art Circus Education

Yorkshire Art Circus, School Lane, Glasshoughton, Castleford, WF10 4QH

We offer module-based practical support for local people. Please send for our brochure.

Art colleges and Adult Education Centres offer a variety of courses, including book binding.

General Information

Your local library will be a gold mine of advice and information.

This is also the place where you can find the most up-to-date copies of *Writers' & Artists' Yearbook*, *Writer's Handbook* and *The Bookseller.*

Arts Funding and Support

For local projects your local authority or parish council might be able to help.
The Arts Council can put you in touch with your own Regional Arts Board.

Arts Council of England
14 Great Peter Street
London, SW1P 3NQ

Scottish Arts Council
12 Manor Place
Edinburgh, EH3 7DD

Arts Council of Wales
Holst House
9 Museum Place
Cardiff, CF1 3NX

FORMS

We have included filled-in sample forms to show you how to use them.

Sample Design Brief:

Here are the specs for

The Book Starts Here
How To Publish Your Story

theme of the book:	guide to self-publishing
dimensions:	2/3 A4, landscape
extent of text:	84 pages, 110gsm paper
cover ideas so far:	a full colour image of Snakes and Ladders, original supplied with brief, background colour, yellow?
wording on cover:	
front:	**The Book Starts Here** **How To Publish Your Story** **Reini Schühle & Karl Woolley**
back:	blurb as enclosed
house style stripe:	yellow? - this can be 'tweaked' so the colour agrees with the artwork.
logos:	YAC
bar code:	yes
cover price:	£6.50
Deadline for designer:	15 July 1996

BOOK SPECIFICATION

date: ....

title: ....

cover: ....colour cover (artwork supplied/artwork rough)

230 gsm metsacard - gloss laminated........matt laminated.......

cromalin proof: ....

cover quantity: ....

run-on of cover on 135 gsm art paper ....

print run: ....

run-on: ....

paper: 100..............115..............gsm matt art/cartridge

number of pages: ....

run-on of extra pages: ....

book size: A5vertical...........A5horizontal..........2/3 A4........................

typesetting: supplied on 3.5" disk (PageMaker 4 or 5, outputted by printer

binding: perfect bound /burst bound/ section sewn

end pages: ....

colour printing: ....

photographs: ....black and white

....colour

illustrations: ....

delivery (please specify

turnaround time) ....

Please send reply to:

Subscription Form

Special Offer to early subscribers

The Book Starts Here - How To Publish Your Story

Are you writing your story - or perhaps you have completed it - and are you looking for ways of getting published?

Discover the ins and outs of copyright, imprint, print runs, news releases, design, royalties and ISBN numbers! In our easy-to-read guide we take our readers through the process of publishing, from editing to production and selling.

With a glossary of publishing terms and *Forms and Samples*.

A book to dip into for background information or to use as step-by-step guide to publishing.

Available from October 1996 as a Yorkshire Art Circus book.

To secure your copy now, subscribe to our **special pre-launch offer:**

• **Pre-launch subscription £5.00 (inc p&p)**

• Cover price £ 6.50	• perfect bound, full colour, matt laminate cover
• 84 pages	• ISBN 1 898311 24 2

• Published by Yorkshire Art Circus, School Lane, Glasshoughton, Castleford, WF10 4QH
  Phone 01977 603028, Fax 01977 512819

....

I would like to order ....copy/copies of **The Book Starts Here**.

I enclose a cheque for £............... for the **special subscription offer** at **£5.00** per copy. (made payable to Yorkshire Art Circus Limited)

Name...............................   Address..

....

Post Code.....................................

Please send your order direct to Yorkshire Art Circus, fao Clare Conlon.

If you would like to take advantage of the special subscription offer we need to receive your subscription plus your payment before 15 October 1996. We will send you the book promptly on publication.

NEWS RELEASE

From Northern Town to Global Village

When Push Comes to Shove Volume 2 ,

Editors Ian Clayton, Ian Daley, Robert Gates

"There are no barriers in Rugby League, just the reality of a game capable of providing the most profound enjoyment and of triggering the sort of friendship that makes a life worthwhile," says **Ken Arthurson**, Director General of the Rugby Football League International Board, in his afterword to this new book.

When Push Comes to Shove Volume 2 is the companion volume to the book that took both the Rugby League and publishing worlds by storm, a book that stayed in the best-seller lists for 18 months. The book features specially commissioned pieces by writer **Alan Plater**, stories from past great players **Terry Clawson** and **Trevor Foster** and current stars like **Gary Schofield**. Introduction by **Sir Geoffrey Lofthouse MP**, Deputy Speaker of The House of Commons and an afterword by **Ken Arthurson**, Director General of Rugby League's International Board.

When Push Comes to Shove Volume 2 was launched at The George Hotel, Huddersfield, on Friday 10 November 1995.

For more information, and permission to use photographs from the book, please contact Ian Clayton at Yorkshire Art Circus.

Tel : 01977 550401

Fax : 01977 512819

ENDS

ADVANCE INFORMATION

The Book Starts Here

How To Publish Your Story

Reini Schühle & Karl Woolley

• Cover price	£6.50
• Binding	perfect binding/paper
• Cover	Full colour, matt laminate
• Extent	84 pages
• ISBN	ISBN 1 898311 24 2
• Classification	Publishing
• Published	October 1996
• Market	How-to guide to publishing and creative writing
• Published by	Yorkshire Art Circus

• National Distribution by   Yorkshire Art Circus

School Lane

Glasshoughton

Castleford

WF10 4QH

Phone   01977 603028

Fax   01977 512819

Trade Discounts and Terms by negotiation

ADVANCE INFORMATION

The Book Starts Here

How To Publish Your Story

Reini Schühle & Karl Woolley

The easy-to-use guide for people who consider writing their story - or perhaps have completed it - and are looking for ways of getting it published.

In a systematic approach to the art of getting published, we take our readers through the process, from editing to book production and selling.

Readers discover the ins and outs of copyright, imprint, print runs, news releases, design, royalties and ISBN numbers.

With a glossary of publishing terms and *Forms and Samples*.

An informative, easy-to-read book to dip into for background information or to use as step-by-step guide to publishing.

Sample Invoice (Credit Note)*

Name of Company: *Yorkshire Art Circus*

Tax Point: *12 January1997*

Customer Details: *WH Smith, (address)*   Delivery Address:

Account Number: *Smith01*

Title	Quantity	Terms	Cover Price
The Book Starts Here	*3*	*sale or return, 48% discount*	*£6.50*

Amount now due (credited)

£10.14

Terms of Trade: *60 days*

* Make sure that you use this form either as Invoice *or* Credit Note *and indicate clearly which it is. The credit note may need to be accompanied by a cheque for the amount.*

Delivery Note

Name of Company: *Yorkshire Art Circus*   Delivery Address

Customer Details: *WH Smith, (address)*

Account Number: *Smith01*

Title	Quantity
The Book Starts Here	*3*

Received by: .... (signature) ....(print name)
date: *12 November 1996*